THE TIMES

BOOK OF

MODERN MANNERS

TO JEANIE

"CIVILITY COSTS NOTHING
AND BUYS EVERYTHING"

LADY MARY WORTLEY MONTAGU IN A LETTER
TO THE COUNTESS OF BUTE, 1756

THE  TIMES

BOOK OF
MODERN
MANNERS

PERFECT BEHAVIOUR IN
AN IMPERFECT WORLD

JOHN MORGAN

WITH CARTOONS BY JONATHAN PUGH

The Times Book of Modern Manners
Published by
HarperCollins*Publishers*
77-85 Fulham Palace Road
London, W6 8JB

00 02 01

3 5 7 9 8 6 4 2

A catalogue record for this book is available from
the British Library.

ISBN 0 72 301070 6

Printed and bound in Great Britain by
Omnia Books, Glasgow

CONTENTS

FOREWORD

'What was it like to know John Morgan?' is the question people have most often asked me since John's death in July of this year. Each Saturday thousands of readers of The Times divined from his weekly advice column on modern manners that he was a person of exceptional wisdom and warmth. While his column appeared effortless, it was John's extraordinary journalistic achievement to be able to smuggle himself into the lives of readers so that they did not merely read him each Saturday but felt they intimately knew him.

This was all the more extraordinary because his column was barely three years old. In that short time he had become a national institution, the obvious person for radio and television - and The Times itself - to turn to when there were sticky questions of etiquette to answer.

The column was invented for him. In the fifty years since the war there have been great changes in Britain. Deference has given way to a rough-and-ready democracy where everyone feels themselves to be of equal worth; proper behaviour, at first ridiculed, has made way for a matey form of American informality. Private morality has changed, too. There are many more divorcees, many more single parents, many more homosexuals unafraid to declare that they are gay.

But with this social revolution has come confusion. When the rules of good manners were fixed and universal, everyone knew what they should be wearing, how they should be behaving. But the modern world has revealed new social dilemmas as the avalanche of readers' letters to John revealed.

It would have been easy enough to winkle out some reactionary backwoodsman to lay down the law, but it would not have been right for Times readers, who need more than mere proscription. What I knew about John Morgan was that he not only knew exactly how to behave, but that he cared enough about the subject to take seriously those who needed some guidance.

There was, for John, no simple answer. Good manners in one place among one set of people could easily cause awkwardness among another. He was intrigued by the troublesome social occasion and his guiding spirit was a desire to minimise offence all round, while allowing as many as possible to express themselves in their own way. His first impulse was to think how he would act in similar circumstances.

Much of his good sense was instinctive. To lunch with John Morgan was a special treat, because he went out of his way to make his guest feel truly special. As Belinda Harley, his best friend and mentor, said at his funeral, if you had a 90-year-old stone deaf dowager to dinner, the best thing would be to sit her next to John, safe in the knowledge that he would work to ensure that she had a good time. He was a gossip, but was never malicious. He liked to inquire but not to intrude. He said kind things without seeming to flatter. And he was as perfect a guest as he was a host.

Now we are left only with John Morgan's words of advice, collected here, which will capture for ever the uncertainties and anxieties of the turn of our century.

NICHOLAS WAPSHOTT
EDITOR, THE SATURDAY TIMES

7

ACKNOWLEDGEMENTS

I would like to thank Nick Wapshott, Editor of *The Times* on Saturday for kindly inviting me to contribute *Modern Manners* to his paper; my literary agent, Belinda Harley, and my amanuenses Jeanie Maby, Charlotte Wilton-Steer and Arabella Battle for making the book happen. Most of all I would like to offer sincere thanks to the army of kind, patient and immensely helpful experts who contribute their specialist knowledge so generously to the column; and last, but certainly not least, the readers of *The Times* for their splendid letters.

INTRODUCTION

I t is with enormous pleasure that I introduce the first *Times Book of Modern Manners*: a short volume, based on my weekly correspondence column. Since *Modern Manners* began in 1997, I've been often amused, sometimes amazed and only very rarely appalled by the sheer diversity of letters cascading over my desk. *En masse* they paint a fascinating picture of Britain today: a nation that both enjoys its traditions but also relishes experimenting with innovations in behaviour. Every letter provides a humorous yet pithy vignette of our contemporary cultural kaleidoscope. Every letter, moreover, shows that the candle of good behaviour burns brightly across the country.

Thus, it was only a matter of time before I would collate the correspondence into a book: indeed, requests for such a volume were coming in from the earliest days. It was decided not just to produce an anthology, but instead to pick the best letters and group them into chapters that cover distinct aspects of our life. To this, I have added extra text and Jonathan Pugh has done some delightful drawings. We both hope that you enjoy our approach.

This combination will enable you to traverse the modern manners minefield successfully and entertainingly. We shall cover the importance of first impressions; codes for childhood; the etiquette of engagement, marriage, separation, divorce and remarriage; the obsequies of death; the polite practicalities of parties, great and small; the nuances of the table; the behavioural bureaucracy of the office; the taming of technology; the semaphore of sexual diplomacy; the perfecting of penmanship; the manners of dress; the etiquette of travel; and finally, a pot-pourri of singular delights.

I trust that you will enjoy reading this book, and that it might encourage you, if you haven't already, to submit a letter to *Modern Manners*. It is you, my correspondents here and abroad, who are the life blood of the column, and the inspiration of its unique style and seemingly lasting appeal. I look forward to hearing from you.

JOHN MORGAN
LONDON, MAY 2000

CHAPTER I

FIRST
IMPRESSIONS

To kiss or not to kiss? That is now the question. How things have changed since Jane Austen etched her gentle heroines onto the national consciousness. Then, outside the safe enclosure of family and dear friends, a kiss was a rare, intoxicating and often long-anticipated event. Nowadays we kiss as if we are an endangered species. The social kiss, once the salaam of the bohemian is now the salutation of Middle England. How displeased Lady Catherine de Bourgh would be.

In Lady Catherine's time, and indeed until very recently, we were more circumspect with our greetings: all the more time to gain artfully an accurate impression. Traditional manners took into account that people, particularly the diffident British, were shy souls who welcomed a protocol that governed primary encounters. This, like its near relation, the etiquette of cards and calling, has gone the way of the dance programme, to be replaced by those touchy-feely modern innovations - the happy hug and the social kiss.

Sadly, far from making the populace relaxed and friendly, the social kiss, as the *Modern Manners* post bag reveals, has generated considerable confusion. Is it correct to kiss, rather than to offer a stiff old handshake: if it is acceptable, is it one kiss or two, and what does well-meaning *moi* do if one's osculatory advances are rebuffed? All these topics have been covered in the column, but the following enquiry is typical of this intimate imbroglio:

Q **I am in confusion as concerns the greeting kiss of the British. The double kiss comes, I am told, "from abroad", and on greeting foreign potentates, seems used to convey great bonhomie if little affection. It has, unfortunately been adopted by the British smart set as de rigueur of course.**

My problem is that, expecting the double kiss, how am I to avoid kissing air, like a hungry chick, or covering a collar with lipstick, when the kisser has sharply turned away his head, having decided that a single peck is sufficient? The indecision of what type of kissing to expect frequently engenders a clash of spectacles. A small collision is generally camouflaged by embarrassed giggling and shaky apologies, whereas a heartfelt, head-on smacker can cause damage and even pain. The solution would be to ban double kissing, a vote-catcher for the Euro-sceptics perhaps? I await your tactful reply but advice to take off spectacles will not be thought sufficient.

A *As a woman, the initiative of "to kiss or not to kiss" resides with you. Thus, at every social greeting make a split-second decision on whether it is to be one, two (left to right is the usual sequence) or none. If you are experiencing problems of your double whammy overtures being unexpected, stick to the simple security of one perfectly formed, affectionate peck on the left cheek.*

Indeed, one correspondent resident in the sophisticated stucco of Maida Vale - an *environs* both louche and cosmopolitan, and where one would think the battle of the social kiss had been won - wrote requesting a complete and exact guide to social kissing. Thus after a considerable amount of research and development, we were able to provide the perfect formula: left, right but not left again, and all with the minimum of human contact. Saliva should never be seen or heard in polite society.

Despite this, there remain many people, apparently often with dark fears about dubious hygiene, who do not welcome the custom. It came as no surprise to receive the following letter from Calvinist *Auld Reekie*, where the mores of Morningside still persist amidst Cool Caledonia.

Q **I read with interest your guidelines on social kissing. My question, writing as someone who loathes the habit, is how can I avoid these unwanted assaults?**

A *You are not alone. I know a Hong Kong hostess who wore a large cage-like hat to deter kissers at her Chinese New Year party. I'm afraid it is not polite to refuse a social kiss, although subtle body language can act as a strong deterrent. On meeting, immediately shake hands, with just enough tension in your elbow to discourage the other person from lunging. Keeping your head quite vertical will reinforce the message.*

Handshaking, of course, is used to transmit many messages ranging from memberships of mysterious organisations to the conveyancing of coded signals, both of an espionage or sexual nature, and sometimes both! The handshake, like many of our ancient customs, has proved remarkably resistant to extinction. And, although many of the traditional protocols of a man always allowing a woman to offer her hand first are now adhered to by only the older generation (modern manners suggest that there should be no hanging around when introductions are made), handshaking still echoes the mores of our medieval past. A man is still judged by how he shakes hands. Indeed, one well-known contemporary comedian was heard to opine that the harsher the handshake, the greater the physical shortcomings elsewhere. Such an observation may bring a wry smile to the face of this correspondent.

Q How should one respond to the 'bone crusher' handshake? To merely remain 'firm' can be painful, or appear wimpish. The best defence is to apply the same force, but this seems to encourage competitiveness in what should be a sign of goodwill.

A *One shouldn't respond at all, as any reaction could be taken as a criticism. Certainly it is not good form to wince, although a well-mannered handshaker never inflicts pain, particularly to ring-wearing women. It is also polite not to try to equal the fierceness of the grip for fear of finding yourself engaged in a social activity akin to genteel arm wrestling.*

The making of introductions is a source of modern-day social angst. In a society that pretends that precedence no longer exists, yet still recoils at causing offence (after all there can't be a nation that says "sorry" as much as we do), people get into a terrific muddle when making introductions. In my work as an image consultant, I have often had to write out the following social mantra onto a small piece of card, which my principal could have at his or her easy reference: "men are always introduced to women, and juniors to seniors". There are, however, occasional exceptions to this rule; for instance, it is probably not politic to present the President Emeritus to the junior secretary. Of course, for the timid the introduction can be just the start of a conversational assault course.

Q How can I avoid uncomfortable silences after making introductions at a party?

A *Immediately after introducing people, follow up with a short biographical detail such as, "Peter has just been to Antarctica" or, even better, say something that establishes common ground between guest and host, for example: "Peter and I met when we had holiday jobs as male strippers".*

Of course, it is not just when we meet each other face to face that problems ensue. In this age of mass communication and melting-pot culturalism, misunderstandings rebound everywhere, from land lines to cyberspace. It seems that unless one possesses the simplest of names (even I, who have, still encounter problems) first impressions can be very treacherous indeed. The following letter is particularly germane:

Q I get into a lot of socially awkward situations because of my Pakistani name, which the English have a great deal of difficulty in pronouncing. Problems occur on the telephone and during social introductions. I often receive mail addressed to Ms Sayed. At school, I was once sent for a medical check-up at an all-girls centre because the officials thought I was female. In a typical telephone conversation if I mention my name, the response is usually "pardon?", and then I have to repeat my name and spell it out. This is embarrassing in an open-plan office, where such dialogue usually causes sniggers by other staff. At times I have to specify that it is Mr. Sayed speaking, e.g. "Could you please ask Mr. Bloggs to call Mr Sayed?". This is to avoid confusion over the gender, but it does sound very pompous. How should I deal with getting my name and sex across in these situations?

A *People can be incredibly cretinous about the spelling of a name far less unusual than yours. For this reason I suggest that you automatically spell out your name each time you give it. It is not good form for you to refer to yourself as 'Mr So-and-so' in speech. However, I assume that the pitch of your voice must give some indication of your sex. If it does not, perhaps you should adopt a baritonal resonance to your voice to dispel any confusion in the future. As far as letters are concerned you might like to inscribe on your business stationery "from Mr Rizwan Sayed", which would leave only the blind in any doubt of your gender.*

This correspondent, Mr Sayed, luckily has time to work on the impression he wishes to give to the world. This luxury, however, is in short supply in everyday life. Psychologists tell us that we gain the bulk of our opinion of a new person within seconds of meeting them. These moments are thus precious, and our manners can quite literally be regarded as social smiles. Smile (obviously not in the manic way favoured by a certain political leader) and the world will smile back at you. Facial twinkles are very much the order of the day in the following illustration of a chance encounter:

Q Could you advise me on the question of procedure when the person in an adjoining seat at a theatre or cinema falls soundly asleep during the performance? Knowing they are on their own, should I nudge them, and thus appear to be making their acquaintance, should I wait until they wake and offer a synopsis of the part missed, or should I leave them snoring gently, hoping their head does not fall on to my shoulder?

A *Leave him be unless his behaviour becomes a public nuisance, for example serious snoring. Sacrilegious as it may seem, as those of us who have regularly attended Glyndebourne (particularly the soporific old house) can testify, certain rather tired patrons enjoy a gentle snooze, particularly after the interval. Much as I would consider this response inherently impolite to the performers and would decry any distracting conduct that interferes with the enjoyment of others, a theatre-goer, as a*

*renter of the seat, is within his rights to do more or less what
he wishes within the limits of civilised behaviour. Sit back,
enjoy the show and pity him for the joys he is missing.*

Missing out is indeed the price of making a poor impression, whether
it be on a potential new friend, lover or business contact. As Lord
Chesterfield famously said: "do as you would be done by, is the surest
method that I know of pleasing." The Earl, as ever, gives good advice.
Today, just as in the eighteenth century, to be struck off someone's
social consciousness is an unnecessary own goal. Only the socially-
challenged need apply.

Chapter II

A Manner Rude and Wild

So to children's manners: a subject which to many might seem oxymoronic. In reality it is merely one of the more challenging and enjoyable aspects of writing *Modern Manners*, where I aim to chart a middle ground through the traditional proprieties of good form and contemporary innovations in behaviour.

This being said, there can be few other areas of correct form that so test the metal of the modern etiquette expert. Although we have come a long way from the old-fashioned definition of a baby as "a loud noise at one end and no sense of responsibility at the other", there has been a shift of emphasis in the relative values of the adult world versus the realm of childhood.

At one time the pecking order was clear: A for adult came before C for child in the alphabet, and such an analogy was enacted exactly in everyday life. As the writer Jill Tweedie recalled of her pre-war childhood: "any child with sense knew you didn't involve yourself with the adult world if you weren't absolutely forced to. We lived on our side of the great divide and we crossed it at our peril."

Nowadays the peril has shifted. Thanks to social changes that a cynic might describe as a new and insidious infantilism of society, while the progressive would put forward as enlightened views on child rearing, the grown-up is often expected to defer to the perceived needs of the child. The result is a contemporary battle field of strongly-held views and culturally-relative prejudices. Yet everyone agrees that childhood needs a social contract. It is not only the Jesuits who believe that the first seven years of life are the most crucial for a child's future development. Educationalists, child psychologists and all sensible parents agree that without proper social training, children enter the grown up world at a disadvantage. Predictably, the pages of *Modern Manners* are in the vanguard of this national debate on junior style and substance.

Questions of style weigh heavily on people's minds long before the arrival of a new baby. What shall we call it? How will we dress it? How will we announce it? These are all regular dilemmas. These are issues in which fashion plays an important role, and just as there is a trend for assuming that your child is the most fascinating creature ever to be born, there is a vogue for sending out extremely important birth announcements, as the following enquiry reveals:

Q My wife and I are expecting our first child, and being the post-yuppies that we are, wish to have a proper birth announcement printed, rather than one of the fill in the blanks-type affairs we have seen. However, we aren't sure of the proper wording, the size, colour and weight of the paper stack, printing v. engraving etc.?

A *The card, which can either be flat or tented, should be made of fairly stiff board (around three hundred and thirty-five grams) and measure either four by three, or five and a half by three and a half inches. It is engraved (never thermographed), with copper plate script announcement: "Mr & Mrs Philip Hardy are happy to announce the birth of a son/daughter". A small card bearing the baby's first name and date of birth is attached with a piece of coloured ribbon: blue for boys, pink for girls, and a non-gender-specific hue for the off-spring of the politically correct are popular choices at the moment.*

Godparenting is another fashionable activity. At one time, godparents were quietly and seriously chosen to literally guide a child's piety: the provision was usually just two godfathers and one godmother for a boy and vice versa for a girl. Now godparenting, thanks to the disintegration of the nuclear family, is a growth industry. It is not uncommon for infants of ambitious parents to be bestowed a platoon of godparents to mentor their little darlings through the vicissitudes of life. Celebrity, wealth, and a wise and giving nature are today the prime criteria for those who aspire to a little surrogate parenting. Nevertheless, being a godparent should carry strong responsibilities as well. One serial godparent, who takes her role very seriously, tells me that at any one time you will be expected to be a psychoanalyst, big sister and safe haven in times of turmoil. I would also hope that good godparents teach manners to their small charges. In this way, one would hope they will not end up as the following disgruntled correspondent:

Q I write as one of a group of godparents who happened to be discussing the acknowledgement, or lack of it, of presents given to our godchildren. It appeared that there is an increasing tendency to non-acknowledgement and this we regard as bad manners. We will be grateful if you can suggest a solution to a problem which has an application perhaps to all ages and especially so at this time of year.

A *The usual method is for the disgruntled giver to the ask the parent of the child "Did Horatio like his Tonka truck? I only ask because we haven't heard from him". Such a course often shames the parents into encouraging Horatio to pen an appropriate letter of appreciation. Should this not work, you could, depending on the relationship enjoyed with the parents, follow the example of an exemplary godparent who, in addition to the usual roles of guiding his godson's piety and offering a general mentoring service, has transformed himself into a self-appointed Lord Chester-field figure charged with proffering occasional social instruction on a variety of topics including the importance of thank-you letters. Little Horatio is doing very well.*

It is not just eighteenth century peers who can be relied upon for sound social counsel. Their descendants are alive and kicking in the *Modern Manners* post bag, and often the source of excellent advice offered in response to my answers in the column. One such is this obviously highly effective way of dealing with socially-anaesthetised godchildren:

Q **Re the failure of godchildren to say thank you for gifts: my mother-in-law's remedy was the best I have come across. After the second absence of a letter she wrote on the next occasion saying that because she knew her godchild was not the sort of**

person to forget a thank you letter she was afraid that the gift must have been lost in the post, and in such precarious circumstances she would not risk sending again. She had a letter and apology by return, and this habit continues.

A *Thank you so much for sending in this ingenious suggestion, which I am delighted to share with our readers. I see a grateful nation resolving to use your method, no doubt to great success, in the coming year.*

The war of the thank-you letter is not the only generational battle of childhood. Another is the dilemma of whether children are automatically included in a social invitation. One correspondent from a sleepy hollow in the Thames valley wrote stating that, although in his opinion infants were always welcome, what about older children? I replied that children of any age are never included by right in a grown-up invitation.

Family holidays can be another inter-generational war of wills, where behaviour veers from sunny to stormy on the spectrum of human behaviour. Here is a very amusing letter from a London cleric with which many readers who are parents might empathise:

Q **Our family is taking a holiday in France, and on the way home we are staying in a bed and breakfast we know. It is owned by an extremely friendly husband and wife team who eat dinner with their guests. Monsieur is a retired Parisian** chef and does the cooking. Last year we had a *haute cuisine* meal that we enjoyed, but it was too sophisticated for our four children, then aged from thirteen to eight, who left most of it. They would much prefer something like chicken nuggets or burgers with chips, followed by ice-cream. Could we suggest in advance the provision of an alternative menu or should we accept the situation for fear of giving offence?

Accept gracefully. Otherwise, not only would you be offending les patrons, *but you would also be wasting an opportunity to broaden your children's culinary horizons. It is not desirable either nutritionally or socially to allow children to assume that convenience foods are the norm, or to forego a marvellous opportunity for them to discover that there is a sensory universe beyond the limited compass of burgers and chips. If you are convinced that your children are going to be difficult you could suggest that their food is cooked more simply. However, I feel that this is a good opportunity to educate your children in the good manners of eating whatever is put in front of them, for, as we all know, children who are over-indulged at the table tend to grow up into dietetically tiresome adults.*

But what of other cultural habits? Although it is relatively easy to develop a palate for unusual foods, exotic customs can be more challenging for the faint-hearted:

Q A cousin lives with, and has young children by, a wealthy and charming Arab gentleman, long resident in this country. The "consort" has a habit of kissing my 13-year-old son upon arrival and departure. My son does not seem to mind, but he is about to enter a major public school, where my cousin's father, brother and I were educated. The intention, I believe, is for their own son to join the same house at this school and this is likely to entail visits and further kissing. Are you against the idea of this kissing and, if so, how would you set about tactfully bringing it to an end?

A *I am not. Times have changed since Winston Churchill kissed his old nanny at Harrow and one of his fellow school boys opined, "that is one of the bravest things I have ever seen". Today's fathers aim to be loved, rather than feared and respected, and many of our top schools have become so international that children are increasingly sophisticated about foreign customs. This, coupled with a more relaxed attitude to social kissing between men, means that your son is unlikely to be embarrassed.*

The word "sophistication" in this reply is perhaps the key to children's modern manners. The days are long gone when blanket obedience was the expected response from minors. Today we understand that we must respect our children as sophisticated beings. However, it is a mistake to believe that they are quite as worldly as they might appear. Children learn from example, whether it be the simple protocol of saying please or thank you, or learning proper table manners. They should be, just as Nanny said, "not at home to Mr. Rude".

CHAPTER III

HOLY
DEADLOCK

Weddings can be such vexing things; both hugely satisfying and vastly daunting; predictable and perplexing; often magical, sometimes grisly in their pretension. Either way, they are always an event in which people who might otherwise claim their lives to be etiquette-free zones are happily willing to embrace its strictures and idiosyncrasies for a successful day. Certainly they form the single biggest section of my mail bag.

Weddings are also one of the great contradictions of our age. The less that the married state remains the bedrock of society, the more time, money and effort we are willing to put into the wedding itself, despite the fact that government figures reveal that nowadays fewer people choose to marry and those that do marry don't seem to do it for very long, at least with the same spouse. The world might be changing, but human optimism and love of ritual are always with us.

Perhaps one of the most challenging dilemmas posed to many modern brides and grooms is how to incorporate the numerous complexities of today's extended family: how to cope with the difficult step-mother, the divorced father who now has a boyfriend, and the possibly rocky road caused by long-divorced parents reuniting to host the nuptials of their daughter. The following query, which arrived in only the second week of the column, is typical.

Q I am getting married next year and my parents are divorced. I get on well with both my father and step-father (who brought me up from the age of nine). I don't want to hurt anyone's feelings, and would like both to participate fully in my wedding. What do you suggest?

A *How lucky you are to have such a happy "step situation". Usually the parents of the bride reunite to host the nuptials of their offspring. Thus, wedding invitations should be issued in the names of your actual father and mother (she is styled by her current married name); your father should give you away and also witness the signing of the register. Your step-father should be offered a key moment in the service, such as reading the lesson. He also needs a role at the reception, and I would suggest you might like to invite him to give the first speech (traditionally reserved for an old family friend) that introduces the bride to the groom's side. If your reception is to be a sit-down affair, it would also be a flattering gesture for him to be given an important table to host. Finally, do remember to allow him to bring a companion (perhaps a sibling) to the wedding to avoid the chilling feeling of social isolation that can lead to trouble on such occasions.*

Some people are not so fortunate, particularly when the various interested parties in the wedding arrangements, the bride's parents, the groom's parents, and the bride and groom themselves, squabble about whose friends will comprise the final make-up of the list. The reasons for this are two-fold. Firstly, the emphasis has shifted from the old idea of a wedding being less of a union between two families towards more of a mega party given by the bride and groom for their friends: the modern ceremony often hovers uneasily between these two poles. A sensible contemporary compromise is to split the list into three: one third for the bride's side, one third for the groom's and one for the friends of the happy couple themselves. After all, today's bride is much more likely to feel closer to her secretary whom she sees every day than to a distant aunt whom she has not seen since childhood. Secondly, the increased pooling of resources, often in families where offspring are better off than the parents, has meant the old paternal rites have diminished alongside paternalistic responsibilities, as the questions below explain:

Q We have paid a large contribution towards the cost of our son's wedding reception but, much to our dismay, have been given no chance to seat our friends and relatives in the way which we should have liked. Do we just agree with the bride's mother's organisation (we should hate to upset either bride or groom) or do we make our requests known?

A *You are right to feel upset. Nowadays there is more pooling of resources when it comes to paying for weddings, and this has brought with it an appropriate sharing of priorities. This does not mean that the bride's parents' role as hosts should appear in any way diminished, but just that those who have contributed ought to be consulted. Therefore I recommend that you make your requests known. But do it gently and perhaps through a third party such as their son: their actions could suggest embarrassment at accepting funding from your side.*

The trend for ever more elaborate weddings has brought a creeping commercialism which, rather like the conspicuous consumption surrounding Christmas, sometimes tends to obscure the real meaning of the ceremony. This manifests itself in many ways, but most unappealingly in the following question:

Q **After deciding to get married after several years living together, and accumulating all the trappings: toaster, kettle, teapots etc., would it be bad manners to invite monetary donations instead of gifts, and how would one politely suggest it in the invitation cards?**

A *One wouldn't. It is in very poor taste indeed to solicit cash instead of presents unless the money is going to charity, such as after a death when mourners are asked to contribute to the loved one's favourite cause rather than sending rafts of flowers. Certainly at a wedding it would be most inappropriate. Instead, draw up a really imaginative wedding list comprising lots of life's little luxuries, ranging from the finest linen sheets to fabulous soaps; items that you have always coveted but have not quite been able to treat yourself to.*

As weddings have increased in their elaboration, the trend has grown for couples to video their weddings. The decision as to whether videos are appropriate lies entirely within the gift of the clergyman concerned, and thus it is polite and practical to ask him if he minds. Attitudes vary enormously from those who are happy to embrace technology to those who forbid it entirely. There is one incumbent of a popular London parish who only allows videoing from a specific vantage point; if the cameraman dares to move, he stops the service. The moral is always to ask early on in the planning stage of the wedding to avoid the difficulties described in the following letter.

Q **I am getting married in September and wish for the service to be videoed. However, at the second meeting with our vicar, it seemed that he does not allow services to be taped. I found this out quite by accident as he did not volunteer such information at our first interview. I am therefore very upset, as I had already booked the video man and paid a deposit. Is there anything that can be done about this, for example, moving the service to a different church? Had I found this out at the third meeting with the vicar a few days before the ceremony, I don't think that I would have been in a fit state to go though with it; I am that upset. I think that vicars should have a duty to tell their prospective wedding couples exactly what they will and won't allow. The vicar did ask us if we had any questions the first time we went, but we were so naive that we did not know which questions to ask.**

A *Churches are holy spots not places of public entertainment to be treated as photogenic back drops. Your vicar is not alone in his sensitivity to the Hollywood approach to the wedding ceremony, and is*

*under no statutory obligation to allow filming in his church.
It is an imperative courtesy for couples to ask and not
assume that videos are acceptable to clergymen. I'm afraid
you rather missed the moment at your first meeting, and to
try and change churches could be problematical and will
appear ungracious. Why not compromise and ask him to
allow the proceedings to be sound recorded and later used in
a video (or even a CD ROM) made up from other images of
the day.*

Children are another difficult area. Modern attitudes to parenting,
combined with the long working hours of couples who, quite
understandably, like to spend all their possible remaining recreational
time with their offspring, have led to the assumption that their little
darlings are always welcome at weddings: unfortunately this is often
not the case. Although there is an increased fashion for "family"
weddings where torrents of tinies are welcome, there are still many
couples who either restrict the presence of children to those of the
immediate family and to those taking part in the service, or who don't
want any children at all. In all cases the wishes of the bride and groom
are to be respected.

Q My wife and I have been invited to a friend's
wedding and reception, but our children
(aged two and four) have not. To enable us to
go we will have to be away two nights. While accepting
that this is their special day and they can invite whom
they want, we feel unable to go without taking our

children. Would it be impolite to reply saying "We very much look forward to coming to the wedding, but as we are unable to find anyone to look after our children, we will not be able to come to the reception"?

A It most certainly would be. If the bride and groom were able or wished to accommodate children they would make it known. It is unkind of you to impose your wishes and to make them feel guilty at an already stressful and busy time. You must decide which is more important to you: sharing their big day, or spending it with the children as usual. They have paid you the honour of inviting you to their wedding. Surely you can repay the compliment by organising child-care?

The other modern complexity is the exact social status of non-married partners when it comes to drawing up a wedding guest list. At one time, except in very rare cases, only married spouses were automatically included in a wedding invitation: other personal arrangements were not. The modern bride, like her forebears, obviously needs to restrict her list, but unlike the bride of yesteryear she has to take account of long-standing couples of all sexual persuasions, as the following letter illustrates.

Q A friend who lives abroad invited me to his wedding without inviting my live-in partner of many years, whom both he and his then fiancée had met more than once. However, he invited another mutual friend with his wife, although he had not met this friend's wife. Discreet enquiries revealed that non-married partners were not invited to keep numbers down. I politely declined the invitation in the usual manner, but privately expressed to my friend that although I would not see him at his wedding, I looked forward to seeing him when he was next in my home city. After I declined the invitation, several mutual friends criticised my decision. I realise that it is entirely in the gift of the bride and groom and their families to give out invitations. However, I feel that in today's society, it is not really acceptable to exclude people's long-term live-in partners simply because they are not married, if numbers are to be kept down. What do you think?

A *I think you are right to feel aggrieved. Although all brides have to create a system to ration their numbers, and living together is only a private arrangement between two people and not the public and legal affirmation of a bond that distinguishes marriage, your friend could have made the distinction between long-term partnerships, which are de facto almost socially equal to marriages, and more short-term arrange-ments, which are not, and do not need to be acknowledged socially at important occasions such as weddings and other celebrations of our rites of passage.*

One of the biggest social trends over the last few years is the increased incidence of marriages across traditional religious and racial barriers. At one time a Christian tended to marry a Christian, a Jew wed a Jew, and the Asian religions were particularly strict in their view of the nuptial state. Nowadays, although it would be wrong to assume that faith and blood differences play no part (their roles are, in fact, far greater that many modern-thinking young people like to imagine), there is an unprecedented rise in mutlicultural marriages. This, of course, provides problems of its own, with usually no accepted convention that the protagonists can fall gratefully into. The result is a whole new set of protocols to cope with individual circumstances, as we read now.

Q Our son is getting married to a Chinese girl who lives in Hong Kong. They are returning to this country for a Church of England service and reception. A week later a Chinese tea party and a celebration dinner will take place in Hong Kong. The bride's parents will fund the Chinese celebrations and we the English. Is it correct for both invitations, to the two ceremonies, to be issued in the name of the bride's parents only?

A *The Hong Kong side of the celebration should follow the Chinese custom which lays down that, although the groom's side usually pays for a wedding, the names of both the bride's and groom's parents appear as joint hosts on the invitation card. The British side of the festivities is more complex. You could be madly novel and decide that as the bride is Chinese her customs should override native conventions and issue invitations in the names of both sets of parents. However, I always think it is better to adhere to local etiquette, and would recommend that it would be more appropriate to send out invitations in the name of the bride's family alone and thus comply with British tradition. This may appear as if you are getting the thin end of the wedge, but remember that your names will be on the Chinese invitations to the Hong Kong party that the other side is funding.*

Chapter IV

The Triumph of Hope over Experience

Now we enter the Wild West of best behaviour: the previously uncharted territory of how to politely separate, divorce and, possibly, remarry. When I was commissioned to bring that redoutable dowager of a book *Debrett's Guide to Etiquette and Modern Manners* into the modern age I was amused to discover how the old book only devoted a handful of paragraphs to these subjects. My new and up-dated version of this volume, on the other hand, boasts a specific chapter devoted to separation, divorce and remarriage. This development shows not only society's acceptance of these life events as being, if not quite pre-ordained rites of passage, then at least unsensationally normal. It also demonstrates our wish as civilised human beings to create a code, where none existed before, which ensures that often traumatic transformations in life can be managed ensuring minimal disruption at the time, and a comfortable *modus vivendi* thereafter.

One of the major problems of ending a marital life is presenting oneself as a single again. Curiously, although the parties in a divorce can often be extremely focused about the actual terms of the settlement - presumably because they are communicating via lawyers, they can be exceptionally coy about making the necessary social arrangements. Moreover, many people find it difficult to distinguish that separation is quite different socially from divorce. In the former state, people remain married - often with the possibility of reconciliation, while in the latter, the bond has been severed, legally and socially. For this reason, it behoves couples to be clear to their friends exactly what arrangement they are living under, and, if the marriage is over, to let people know. This correspondent's dilemma of how to do this, is, I suspect, typical of many:

Q After much to-ing and fro-ing, soul-searching and legal wrangling, my husband and I have now parted company permanently. I am obviously keen to rebuild my life socially and want to know how to let people know that I am 'footloose and fancy-free'?

A *American-style divorce celebrations are as yet not usual here. A more reticent approach is still considered good form. The most usual device is to let your stationery take the strain. Whichever one of you has left the family home must send out change of address cards which, in addition to the obvious function, will demonstrate how, in the case of a woman, she is to be styled, i.e. Mrs. Lucy Welsh. Christmas cards are also extremely useful for this purpose.*

Judging by the tone of that correspondent, I doubt she will be on her own for long. Soon she may find herself in the position of the following couple:

Q We are getting married (neither of us for the first time) in October with an evening wedding and reception (dinner) at a London hotel. We are paying for the ceremony ourselves. How should we word the invitations? I anticipate having around 80 guests, but only wish a small proportion of them to attend the ceremony (also in the hotel). Should

we word the invitations to invite people to the reception
only and include a note to those we wish to attend the
ceremony, or should I get a card printed separately to
include with the invitation to the reception?

A *You should have two separate cards. The first
should read "Mr. Peter Pink and Mrs Molly
Magenta request the pleasure of your company at
their marriage at The Green Park Hotel on Saturday, 12th
October, at 6 o'clock and afterwards at Dinner". The second
would read "Mr Peter Pink and Mrs Molly Magenta request
the pleasure of your company at Dinner at The Green Park
Hotel following their marriage on Saturday, 12th October, at
7.30 for 8 o'clock.*

Presents are another vexing issue. In a society that sanctions
institutionalised greed, yet still considers such avariciousness bad
manners, there is often much tooth-sucking on what level of
commercialism is considered appropriate for the second or third-time
bride or groom.

Q We are getting married in the summer, both
of us for the second time after previous
marriages of about thirty years each. We will
marry in a registry office privately, and the following
day have a Service of Dedication attended by about one
hundred family and friends, followed by a lunch. We
feel people will probably want to give us some sort of

wedding gift and wonder what would be the correct way of indicating that if they wish there are certain items we would like to receive. We don't feel the normal wedding list is quite appropriate second time round.

A *You are right. Second weddings should never be characterised by the consumerist bonanza that attends a first-time bride. Already well-equipped previously-married couples should be circumspect in their expectations and content themselves with more token presents. It would be poor form to establish lavish lists at department stores and expensive specialist shops. However, you could hit upon a more modest, original idea that would capture your guests' imaginations, such as establishing a list at a book shop of volumes you would like to have in your library.*

One of the great attractions of second weddings is that they can entirely reflect the taste, aspirations and personalities of the bride and groom. This, as we all know, is not always so the first time around when considerations of parental ambitions and family politics often take precedence. Although we have yet to adopt the Stateside standard of serial matrimony, the idea that second wedding celebrations should be small and discreet is fading. As one friend said, "Darling, these days the first wedding is just the rehearsal, it's the second one that is the real thing." For this reason, second-time-arounders can quite suitably see their nuptials as the excuse for a grand gathering.

This wish to celebrate great events properly is all to do with our love of ritual, something that age never withers and that increase in wealth and maturity can aid. Thus it comes as no surprise to learn that the contemporary debate about the acceptability of wedding rings for men is as much a topic of speculation with subsequent spouses as it is with primary ones.

Q I would like your advice on the subject of rings. My partner and I, both divorced, are considering setting up home together, and she has expressed a wish that we should each wear a ring to express our joint commitment. I am demurring on the basis that I am unsure which hand, or finger of the left hand indicates marriage, where one worn on the third finger of the right hand indicates the wearer is single, and therefore available.

A *The correct finger is the third finger of the left hand. Although most usually used by married people, this digit has since ancient times, when it was thought that it contained a vein that led directly to the heart, been the finger that symbolised commitment.*

It is this sense of commitment that people curiously often find confusing and embarrassing. It seems that until we are able to exorcise completely the ghosts from the past, we are unwilling to deal with the social pragmatism of the present. But it must be dealt with, not just for the sake of the people immediately concerned, but for the wider circle as well. In this way, misunderstanding, and its more pernicious sister, gossip, can be minimised.

Q A friend's wedding is giving rise to a great deal of work gossip. We all know that her fiancé is recently divorced with a young child, but she never mentions this and gives the impression that it is a first wedding for them both. Colleagues feel that she is hypocritical and are showing little interest in her plans. My friend is upset by their attitude. Should I try to find an opportunity to explain tactfully what we know, or do I risk losing her friendship as she is a very sensitive person? (Later this year she is to take up a more senior position at work but colleagues feel she is devious and untrustworthy). As the only invited guest to the wedding from work I feel I need some advice on this very sensitive situation.

A *Good manners always recognise a distinction between professional and personal life. Perhaps you are making rather too much of a private matter which really is not office business. As the only invitee you are obviously closer to the bride, who may simply be slightly shy about the fact that her fiancé has been married before. By all means try to bring this into the open tactfully. Your friend will probably be relieved that it need no longer be kept a secret and that there will be no necessity for more gossip. It sounds to me as if there is a certain amount of professional jealousy surrounding her promotion which is getting transferred to her personal circumstances.*

When it comes to widows and widowers remarrying, the past is indeed a ghost. But this does not prevent problems of an altogether more temporal nature arising:

Q *I am a widow in my mid-fifties, and this summer I am going to marry a widower. We are planning a church wedding with a reception afterwards. My parents are still alive, but elderly and infirm. Obviously we hope they will be able to attend the service and reception, but we are not expecting them to take any active part, nor contribute to the cost. Can you please advise me how the invitations should be worded? It would clearly be nonsense to expect my parents to be the hosts, even nominally. Will it be in order for the invitations to be in the joint names of my fiancé and myself? Also, I am an independent woman and have no wish to be given away by anyone. Can this be omitted from the service and, although unconventional, why should not my fiancé and I walk up the aisle of the church together?*

A *Traditionally the widow bride hosted her own wedding with the following wording on her invitation: "Mrs John Smith requests the pleasure of your company at her marriage to Mr. Charles Brown" etc. However, in recent years this has been largely superseded by the bride and her future groom giving the nuptials, with the wording: "Mrs John Smith and Mr Charles Brown request the pleasure of your company at their marriage". Both are correct. As far as your being given away is concerned, you*

*and your swain could enter the church together, but this
arrangement is more usual for blessings than weddings
and, for this reason, you might like to ask a male relation
to escort you to the altar.*

CHAPTER V

DEATH DUTIES

The post-war world brought us antibiotics, increased longevity and the idolisation of youth. These factors all contributed to death becoming known as the last taboo. It was seen as something to be ignored, delayed and almost denied. The rituals that attended the dead, so important to earlier generations, were scaled down to suit this new mood.

In recent years, however, there has been a change of emphasis and although we will not witness a return to the mawkish mourning manners of the Victorians, there is, without doubt, a new morbidity gripping the national psyche. The reasons for this are complex, but can be explained by the demographic increase of an ageing population, for whom death promises to be an imminent reality rather than an abstract promise. This, combined with our crisis of confidence in modern medicine, new and nastier diseases, plus a spate of high profile deaths, have put death and its obsequies back on the social agenda. As Molière said: "You only die once and it's for such a long time."

It would be a mistake to assume that we are just talking about gloom. We are not, and one example of this can be seen in the vast increase in memorial services that now follow people's demises. At one time this rite of passage was largely accorded only to the great and good. They were, as Ralph Richardson remembered: "the cocktail party of the geriatric set", and only grand geriatrics at that. Nowadays, many people enjoy this final and fond farewell since, unlike a funeral which just commemorates a death, a memorial service celebrates the life of the dear-departed.

Whatever form these final services take, it is important for everybody concerned to make an effort. It remains good manners for the living to honour the dead, whether it be by sending flowers or, as the following letter reveals, making sure to wear the right clothes on the day:

Q Apropos funeral etiquette: when closely related and deeply grieving, my feelings tell me how to dress. However, if the relationship is one of more distant family, or of respect or duty, it is more difficult. Is it ostentatious to wear all black, possibly with a touch of white, when so many nowadays don't? Conversely, when one is truly grieving, but is not family, is it presumptuous to dress in this way? Finally, what is correct for women in the matter of jewellery? Without any I feel I might look like an undertaker's clerk. With suitably chosen pieces (a Victorian mourning brooch, family rings), I felt I was honouring my aunt at her recent funeral by according importance to her last public appearance. But was I wrong?

A *No, you are not wrong. Funerals are the last chance for the living to honour the dead. Every effort should be made to do things well, and this includes the dress of mourners. Black, although no longer* de rigueur, *is never incorrect and for obvious reasons remains the most appropriate hue regardless of the mourner's relationship to the deceased. Jewellery can and should be worn, but ought to be simply and sparingly sported, and indeed the pieces that you mention sound absolutely ideal. I'm sure your aunt would have approved.*

Letters of condolence are also areas of disquiet. In an age when the writing of sensitive letters is almost a lost art, mourners sometimes delay putting pen to paper. But write they must. Grief is often tempered by kind letters. For this reason the written style must be sympathetic but not sentimental, should cite a special recollection or observation of the deceased and should be able to stand re-reading. But to whom should these letters of condolence be addressed?

Q **Is it appropriate to write a letter of sympathy to a couple on the death of one of their parents, rather than to just the partner who is the blood relative - especially if they are both known to have been devoted to the deceased?**

A *Condolence letters should always be addressed directly to the blood relation of the deceased. This does not prevent the writer from expressing sympathy to the devoted spouse in the body of the letter. Such sentiments are always greatly appreciated.*

Of course, manners are not a one-way street. Even in death it is important that mourners behave in a polite way towards those who have shown sympathy and care during difficult times. This may seem obvious, but it is extraordinary how people can use grief as an excuse for undue selfishness, as the following letter reveals:

Q **I would appreciate your opinion on the following. My wife and I were on an extended holiday in the States early this year, when we heard that a neighbour and friend of some twelve years had died. We made several long-distance calls and**

arranged for a neighbour to purchase a wreath on our behalf, which was duly delivered. On our return my wife called on the widow to express our sympathy (I failed to do so personally) and since then she has ignored and avoided me. I was also waiting for a thank-you card from her for the wreath. When my first wife died many years ago, I sat for hours writing and thanking everyone for their flowers. Has this little courtesy gone out of style?

A *Absolutely not. It is still correct form to write and thank for all flowers, wreaths and indeed letters of sympathy. I was reminded of this courtesy recently when, on the death of a well-known decorator, I wrote to his widow, whom I had never met, to receive, almost immediately, a letter of appreciation with information about the memorial service. This I considered immaculate mourning manners. As far as the widow's attitude towards you is concerned, I would not lose too much sleep over it. Grief affects people in all sorts of different ways, and she may just need time to return to normal behaviour. Your wife has called and expressed your joint sympathies, so you can feel assured you have been good neighbours.*

It is not just the status of death that has to be considered. The social standing of those left behind also changes. Elder sons inherit titles, daughters become heiresses and, as women tend to out-live men, there are battalions of widows enjoying lonely lunches in sunlit dining rooms. These women, once they have put aside their widows' weeds, and adjusted to being on their own, are often unsure about their social obligations. If I had a pound for every letter that has been sent to the column asking about whether a widow should be styled with her own first name or that of her late husband, I would be a very rich man indeed. The answer is that widows continue to use their husband's Christian name, and remain for example, Mrs. William Woebegone, and not, as many people believe, Mrs. Wilma Woebegone, which is an epithet used for divorcees.

And what of the ring? This symbol of eternal love and devotion continues to be worn until a widow either remarries or dies. But, as the following letter reveals, although death may be final, as one door closes another one surely opens:

Q More on rings please. Should widows continue wearing their wedding rings? I have continued to do so, but when in the company of male friends, strangers have sometimes assumed that we are married. Would it be suitable to wear the ring on my right hand? What about the niceties of signalling availability/unavailability to potential male friends?

A *No, it would not be suitable for you to wear your wedding ring on your right hand, as this could be interpreted as your being committed to Christ in a relationship analogous to marriage, such as belonging to a religious order. This, I'm sure, is not quite the sentiment that you are trying to convey. As far as giving the green, red or even amber light to men, there are far more subtle womanly ways to do this rather than the artful sporting of ironmongery.*

CHAPTER VI

THE TASTE OF SOCIETY

My readers love parties. Whether enthusiastic hosts or over-enthusiastic guests, they relish all aspects of social life: the planning and preparation on one hand and the attending and enjoying on the other. Moreover, whatever they are doing and wherever they are going they are fascinated by the menu of manners and etiquette that regulate social occasions.

The letters to the column provide not only entertaining reading, but an incisive portrait of the nation at play. There is however one leitmotif that links these dinner, drinks or garden parties, and that is a wish to get things right: this in today's Britain means correct but not stuffy, relaxed but not rude.

These factors are at the heart of our national hospitality. As a wag once said: "the French may have etiquette, but the English have good manners". It is this flexibility and charm, plus a long tradition of domestic entertaining that gives our approach to conviviality its very distinctive and delightful flavour.

This is not to presume that our customs are set in stone; they are not. Busy living and increased informality have meant that the great Anglo-Saxon social staple - the formal dinner party - is fast becoming the exception rather than the rule; the free-form all-evening party is these days more popular than the more-regimental traditional 6.30 - 8.30 "stand up and shout", and a code of entertaining prevails that is perhaps more dominated by the sensory pleasures of good food and wine than the strictures of form. Cold food no longer comes with coronets.

The influence of the United States, as on all aspects of our lives, cannot be underestimated. From across the cultural as well as the oceanic divide sprang cocktails, barbecues and hostess gifts. The latter custom is a relic from the austere days of Puritanism, and requires American guests to always take a present if they are invited to friends' houses. This may well have been one of the social planks of the Founding Fathers, but it did not take hold of this country until the 1960s when it became acceptable to bring a small box of chocolates but nothing else. The austerities of the 70's sometimes made it acceptable to take a bottle of wine, and by the 80's all manner of tributes from the floral to the facile were presented to the expectant hostess. This does not mean that this practice is entirely acceptable. The older generation are still sometimes bemused and often insulted by it, and there is no doubt that it is a solecism to arrive gripping a gift at a very formal dinner where evening dress (black or white tie) is to be worn. Yet, in most cases today a present has become, if not *de rigueur*, then a desirable accessory. And with new customs come new conventions.

Q I would be grateful if you could settle a difference of opinion that I have with my wife. When we have guests for dinner they invariably bring small gifts such as bottles of wine and after-dinner mints or chocolates. My wife insists that these should be put to one side and not used during the evening. Her argument is that it would be presumptuous to do so, almost as if we are relying on our guests to complete the preparations for them, insinuating that we have not bought sufficiently for the evening. I have an entirely different view, I think that we should heartily tuck in and sample all that is presented. It may well be that they had chosen the offerings with care and would be disappointed if they were not given the opportunity to try them. Also, giving the impression that we were waiting until they left before scoffing the lot seems rather mean. How do you see the situation?

*A**Hosts are under no obligation to serve anything that their guests bring. The secret of successful entertaining is to have all the elements of a party in place, without counting on possible donations by guests. On the other hand, spontaneous exceptions that will bring pleasure to those present can be made. For instance, should a guest arrive bearing a special little extra that would make an exquisite embellishment to the evening, then it would be a sin not to share it.*

Despite all these external influences it would be a mistake to believe that we have lost our love of ritual. It is a truism to say that we present pageantry better than any other nation, and when we put on a formal dinner there is nothing that can better fabulous silver set on polished mahogany in the expensive and flattering glow of candlelight. On such occasions we dwell much on the pros and cons of *placement*. More correctly called *place à table*, as one senior member of the Royal family is known to remind her less *comme il faut* co-hosts, is still an issue. And, although strict hierarchies that once governed entertaining have faded into a sepia past, it is still true to say that the place of the guest of honour (on the right hand of the host or hostess) is still a coveted position. But where, indeed, should the host sit? This has vexed more than one Times reader:

Q I find nowadays at dinners that the host and hostess often occupy the mid-points on the sides of the table, facing each other, with the guests arranged to the right and left of them in *placement* order. I prefer to sit at the head of my own table with my wife at the other end. Apart from the pleasure it gives me to be able to look down the length of the table - duties to the guests near me permitting - I believe this arrangement leads to a more integrated group, and also makes it easier to spot if any guest has a problem. My wife says I am out-of-date and should change.

A *There is nothing new about hosts and hostesses taking these places at dinner: as a custom it has a long provenance and is popular with the Royal Family. It is particularly useful for very large dinners, as it places the host and hostess and their guest of honour in the heart of the action. However, your wife is wrong when she says that your arrangement is* passé. *It is still, by far, the most usual* place à table *and offers all the benefits you mention. Your house is your castle and I suggest you stick to your preferences.*

Drink, and plenty of it, is an essential part of British entertaining. Foreign nationals, when they are posted here by their companies or embassies are amazed by the amount of booze we put away. No social gathering in this country is complete without a liberal sprinkling of alcohol. As Jerome K. Jerome once said, "we drink one another's healths, and spoil our own". It is thus no surprise that we have a very high instance of alcoholism in our country, and even *Modern Manners*, that pillar of contemporary gentility, has to deal with this modern vice.

Q We are wine lovers and enjoy a glass or two with every evening meal, but we are due to entertain new acquaintances both of whom are attending Alcoholics Anonymous and are doing very well. Should one be sensitive and offer non-alcoholic drinks only and have no alcohol in evidence at the meal, or is this too pointed?

A *Yes. Going teetotal for an evening would be thoroughly counterproductive. Your guests, if they have good manners, will feel awkward about their problem dominating the evening, and remember it is they who have the problem, not you. Moreover, it would make nonsense of the fact that successfully rehabilitated addicts have to live in the real world, which is positively marinated in booze of all kinds. When they arrive, ask in a perfectly normal way, "what may we offer you to drink?" and make sure that there are some tantalising non-alcoholic options. You, however, can tuck into the Chateau Latour, confident that you are being not just good hosts, but happy ones too.*

Perhaps too much Latour is not such a good thing after all. Was it not Dorothy Parker who opined intoxicatingly, "one more drink and I'd have been under the host". Happily such excesses appear rare in the cosy arcadia that *Modern Manners* regulates. Bad wine, however, seems to be an occupational hazard even in the best-regulated of households.

Q **If at a friend's you find the wine offered to be undrinkable, and your host seems blind to this, how can you correctly excuse yourself?**

A *In the first instance just leave it undrunk, perhaps occasionally bringing the glass to your mouth to mimic taking a small sip of the noxious ichor, and hope the host does not notice your reticence. If he does catch on, then the gentlest wheeze is to slip into that social mechanism of last resort: the small white lie. This is something that this column generally tries not to advocate, but occasionally has to sanction in the cause of good relations. Simply say: "Oh I'm so sorry, I took a headache pill before I came out/ I'm on antibiotics at the moment / I'm trying not to drink today and really shouldn't, but thank you."*

Corked wine is a sure way to sink a party. The same is true of ungrateful and badly-behaved guests: those who fail to understand that their part of the social contract is to behave properly and, almost literally, sing for their supper. Sadly, *Modern Manners* is often swamped with sad stories from hosts slighted by guests too selfish to realise that a party is a public activity rather then a private indulgence. Social crimes include arriving late, talking only to the other guest they personally find interesting (to the exclusion of less fascinating creatures) and behaving as if in their own home. This contemporary inability to distinguish between the private and public arena is only too well illustrated by the following letter of the guest who likes to make herself too much at home:

Q When visiting friends' houses for supper or dinner parties, my fiancée has a habit of removing her shoes during the course of the evening. Occasionally she will seek the approval of the hostess before doing so, but more often she will just slip them off, under the table for example. I feel this is somewhat discourteous and that she should at least take slippers or "house shoes" to change into in friends' homes. She is adamant that this is not necessary. Is she committing a social gaffe?

A *She is. Many people in their selfish quest for their own comfort are unable to distinguish between a family occasion and a normal social gathering. Running around barefoot, unless there is a hippie theme to the evening, is not acceptable behaviour. Also taking an alternative pair of indoor shoes, as if visiting a temple, is not common practice in leafy Albion. No, advise her to invest in comfortable shoes, which she should aim to put on and keep on for the entire evening.*

As well as chronicling social mores and prescribing acceptable solutions to behavioural dilemmas, from time to time *Modern Manners* has to innovate in areas where no precedent exists. This we are always delighted to do as the following letter reveals:

Q I find myself at functions which take place in gardens and marquees. The problem is that speeches or toasts often intrude without warning as we are sipping champagne and conversing, inevitably standing away from any convenient surface on which to set down the glass. The result is an embarrassingly feeble ripple of applause as we try not to spill the precious liquid. Some get around this by putting the glass down on the grass, where it usually falls over, or even between their knees, which looks inelegant. Others down the wine swiftly and put the glass in their pocket. I usually hold the glass steady, while flapping my free hand to mime applause, thus showing appreciation without generating a sound. Short of not drinking at all, is there a better way to cope?

A *Having been in your position many times I have perfected my own method of accommodating a glass while not only clapping, but standing up, holding a plate and eating with a fork. The secret is to nestle your left arm closely to your side and cradle the bulb of the glass in the crook of your elbow while resting the base on your left hip-bone. Although this might sound madly precarious it is in fact, with a little practice, remarkably secure, discreet and elegant.*

Sadly, my system turned out to be not as universally secure as I supposed. My innovation, although perfect for men and for flat-chested women is apparently less practical for the generously-busted females, some of whom encountered certain logistical difficulties.

CHAPTER VII

TOP TABLES

Today's manners, like many of the standards of our national life, have been bequeathed to us by the high-minded Victorians and Edwardians. For these forebears the art of gracious living became a vocation that was pursued with a tenacity similar to the enthusiasm that characterised the global expansions of the Empire.

The Empire has gone and many of its social conventions with it, but we should be deeply grateful that one of their great legacies still endures - good table manners. Eating is an essential, but fundamentally unattractive activity: witness a cow chewing its cud and you will instantly understand what I mean. Our great-grandfathers, in their quest to control the natural world, knew this and codified a complicated lexicon of prandial practices that enabled people to deal with any type of edible eventuality, and, therefore, to turn a basic human function into a theatre of grace, charm and practicality.

Of course this bequest has been adapted, some might say squandered, by succeeding generations. Just as we have witnessed a decrease in the level of formality in entertaining (as discussed in the previous chapter), we have seen a corresponding decline in formal table manners. Some might argue that this is a good thing. Who wants to endure a social life that resembles nothing more than a Bateman cartoon? However, there can be little doubt that the table manners of many of the young have deteriorated and only those who wish to be encouraged to diet permanently would want to sit opposite them. Again we find ourselves in the generational cross-fire which characterises much of the debate of *Modern Manners* and, indeed, much of the discussion across the media in general about behaviour. In fact, if there is one single issue that encapsulates this dichotomy it is the elbow problem:

Q Could you please settle a long-standing dispute? My husband was brought up to believe that it shows extremely bad manners to place one's elbows on the table during a meal. He insists on this rule being obeyed by our teenage children, much to their annoyance. While I would normally want to support my husband in the upbringing of our children, I do not see this as a relevant matter to argue over at the dinner table. I notice that it is commonplace for people from all backgrounds to rest their elbows on the table at home, at friends' houses, or even in the smartest of restaurants. Could you please provide the definitive answer, so that peace can reign at our dinner table?

A *Your husband is quite sensible to take a strict line. There are two reasons why elbows on the table are bad news and poor manners: the traditional one, which cites them as ugly barriers to practising the art of conversation, and the modern reason that pre-supposes that children who are allowed to eat in this fashion are liable to develop even more unappealing, sloppy and unsavoury table manners. Surely, clever chat and charming chomping are to be encouraged in the young?*

Indeed, and in everybody else, I say. My main beef with elbows is that they can be conversational barriers. As the great Dr. Johnson said: "there is in the world no more delight (except that of sensuality) but the exchange of ideas in conversation." In this way, good table manners can be seen as facilitators for enjoyment, as it is my sincere belief that such etiquette is inclusive rather than exclusive.

Not knowing the rules can cause embarrassment. This has become particularly evident in the rise of restaurant culture. Individuals who have enough money and culinary sophistication to enjoy an evening out in a fashionable eatery will sometimes find their enjoyment marred by their ignorance of form. There are many anecdotal, and often apocryphal, tales about hapless souls drinking from finger bowls, guzzling garnishes and getting into a terrific muddle with crustacea. Finger bowls, those little refinements, are intended for merely light ablutions at the table. The same is true of hot towels:

Q To my acute embarrassment, my husband, when given a hot towel after a meal proceeds to use it to vigorously wash his face, his expanse of bald head, the back of his neck as well as his hands. I would greatly appreciate it if you would publish this letter and offer your comments.

A *Maybe your husband thinks that he is at the barbers. Hot towels in restaurants are rather like finger bowls, and are intended only for very light ablutions at the table. They are primarily meant for cleaning the hands, but the odd decorous dab of the lips is acceptable.*

However, it must be said that nobody should feel tyrannised by the diktats of the table. Many is the occasion when an evening is completely ruined for timid souls who worry too much about making gaffes. A sad case in point is a little woman attending a formal dinner in the City who, when she was presented with unwanted food, rather than refusing the offending victuals, tipped the entire contents of her plate into her handbag where it languished for several hours. Only people with bad manners will draw attention to mistakes made by those who do not know an accepted mode of conduct, and in the final analysis any diamond, no matter how rough, deserves to enjoy himself.

Q I have a friend who is unaccustomed to eating in restaurants and whose gastronomic tastes are basic. Later this month I am taking him to lunch at a grand establishment in Bristol. I know he enjoys fish and I am concerned that he will order Dover sole with chips, then ask the head waiter for HP sauce or tomato ketchup. How can I prevent this and what should be my response if it occurs? My friend is quite untutored in matters of this nature and I am afraid of causing him offence.

A *I think you should loosen up about your rough diamond. Remember that he is your guest and the restaurant is only providing a service. Sometimes the grandest people have the strangest eating habits and would not think twice about satisfying their whims in a top restaurant or club. If your friend orders bottled sauces with his fish you should indulge him, remembering that the quintessence of good manners is to make the other person feel comfortable.*

The same is true of those with disabilities and injuries, who should not be forced to conform to conventions that might make them feel uncomfortable. Indeed, good manners would expect new codes to be conceived to suit their special needs:

Q **I have recently spent several weeks with my right arm in a sling (I am right-handed). Is there any special etiquette for one-armed people in restaurants? Should the waiter recognise the problem and serve things accordingly? For example, putting drinks down on the left in my case? Or should he avoid drawing attention? Does one ask the waiter or one's partner to cut up one's food?**

A *In a good restaurant the waiter will recommend things that are easy to eat for the one-armed diner. If, however, there needs to be some cutting up, this should be performed by the staff and not at the table, nursery fashion, by dining companions. As far as any readjustment of table furniture - such as moving glasses and spoons to the other side - is concerned, you might have to specify changes but again these are to be performed by staff and not diners.*

However, there are certain tasks that *must* be performed by the diner himself:

Q Occasionally when eating, one finds a piece of gristle or some other unchewable item in one's mouth. What is the correct procedure to adopt: (a) swallow it (b) become a vegetarian (c) take out your handkerchief, giving the impression you are going to clear your nose, but slyly eject the unwelcome object into your handkerchief or (d) lastly and most ingeniously, draw the attention of those with whom you are dining to your admiration of a painting or other features at the other side of the room. Then, while everyone turns to behold this object, swiftly and dextrously remove it from your mouth. How would you score these? Is there a "correct" procedure to adopt in these circumstances.

A *Option one is unpleasant, potentially dangerous and quite beyond the call of good manners unless travelling in primitive societies where the unblinking consumption of unspeakable morsels is a sign of the utmost* politesse. *Alternatives (b), (c) and (d) are unnecessarily convoluted and over-dramatic but have much comic potential. Opt instead for tried-and-tested good form, which like many of the best examples of etiquette is simple and sensible: bring the cupped palm of your left hand to your mouth, discreetly and silently "cough" the offending article into it and deposit it on the side of your plate. No-one should be any the wiser.*

The techniques of how to eat tricky foods seem to have an enduring and neurotic fascination to students of etiquette: the intricacies of consuming foods as diverse as corn on the cob and Dover sole have all been dissected in relentless detail in the column. But it is probably this letter asking how to eat a pear in polite society that gave me the greatest pleasure in explaining this ultimate refinement at the table of the *ton*:

Q I read that "the grandest way to skin a pear is said to be with a teaspoon". I tried this at a dinner party recently, but it did not work and people giggled at my attempts. Where did you come across this arcane notion?

A *I am so sorry that you had problems but I promise you that it is a* bona fide *method. The technique is as follows: choose a large, ripe pear (a nice fat Comice is best) and use as small a spoon as possible. Cut the pear in half crossways (not lengthways avocado-fashion) just under half way down. Starting with the lower, larger half, use the spoon to gently prise the flesh from the skin and eat it. You will be left with two empty skins, the core, and the admiration of all those around you.*

CHAPTER VIII

BEAUTIFUL BUREAUCRACY

Now to modern manners in the workplace for an exploration of contemporary professional protocols. Readers might be excused for thinking that in the piranha pool of modern business, manners are about as much use as a wooden sword to the ancient gladiator in the Coliseum. Happily they are misguided.

It may be true to say that the old corporatist and paternalistic amateur has largely been sacrificed at the altar of ruthless competition and profit margin mania, to be replaced by less savoury individuals for whom good behaviour is not an essential check and balance on the bottom line. However, the clever plutocrat knows the power of politeness. One such paragon of corporate empowerment and princeling of office politics always points out that success in business depends upon: "deploying a feather most of the time, a sword occasionally and a dagger only when absolutely necessary."

This man, and others like him, understand that good manners are part of the great game where confidence, brinkmanship and style (yes, that word again) are key qualities. They understand the pyrrhic victory of acruing unnecessary enemies through rudeness, the pointlessness of making people feel small or putting them needlessly on the spot, and the usefulness of allowing your opponent to think he has got the better of you when he hasn't. The best captains of industry sack people beautifully, top and tail their letters by hand, and know that only little people are late for appointments.

They also have adapted to the relentless blurring of the demarcation between work and leisure. Although, thankfully, we have yet to catch up on the American "I am what I do" school of personal identity, there is no doubt that we are working harder and socialising more than ever in the pursuit of profit. Such a social contract is helped not only by the upholding of traditional courtesy but by the generation of a new set of codes as well. These range from e-mail etiquette to the acceptability of the social kiss at work:

Q I attend business meetings of committees in the City. Several personal friends are members; I find it very awkward when they greet me with a kiss on each cheek. What action do I take with the other members whom I may have only met two or three times? I normally extend a hand for a handshake. I feel kisses are *de trop* at business meetings even with those I know well. What do you think?

A *I agree with you that for the post-modern woman there should be a clear demarcation between personal and professional life, and feel that you are quite justified in resenting oscillatory advances, which although appropriate socially are not nearly so acceptable at work. The secret is to stand ramrod straight and hold out your hand manfully with an elbow of steel when you suspect you are about to be lunged at. Women are very sensitive to these signals and men soon get the message.*

One small but perfectly-formed expression of this new professional puréeing of business and social can be seen in the rise and rise of the business card. This small but potent talisman of the networking culture has virtually obscured its genteel forebear, the visiting card. It has developed its own code of behaviour which can be seen as the modern inheritor of the delicate protocols which regulated the leaving, exchange and reciprocating of calling cards. Customs vary considerably in different countries. For example, when meeting with Japanese business contacts it is polite to offer one's card immediately to every possible person in the room before taking your seat. The card should be offered with both hands and accompanied by a deep bow from the waist. The recipient takes the cards and then has to feign fastidious fascination and read the proffered name for five very long seconds, ending with an "ah so" of deep recognition and appreciation. In the West, things are less stringently encoded but there are conventions. Some people recommend offering cards at the beginning of a meeting to establish a pecking order, and to memorise forgettable names and faces. *Modern Manners*, on the other hand, turned its lizard-like gaze onto the following enquiry and devised an altogether more elegant solution.

Q I am often faced with the uncomfortable decision, upon entering a business meeting, as to when to exchange business cards. Is it correct etiquette to proffer one's card following the initial introductions, at the end of the meeting, just prior to one's departure, or should one only expect to present one's card when asked for it?

A *Cards are best not proffered at initial introductions. Remember that those you are meeting need, and want, to concentrate on you rather than a bit of cardboard. The most appropriate time, unless one has been requested earlier, is at the end of the meeting when you say, "May I give you my card?".*

It would be coy to attempt a chapter on professional manners without discussing the impact of feminism in the work place. Prior to the surge of the feminist sisterhood, it seemed that men were always bosses and women self-abnegating secretaries, and the manners associated with this were based on a creaking chivalric code. The last thirty years have induced a cultural inversion and now women, quite rightly, are bursting through the glass ceiling, like dolphins through the spray of a South Atlantic dawn. Manners, however, like many social issues, take their time to adapt to the seismic shifts in the dialogue of the sexes.

Q I should like to take a step further your recent answer saying that a husband, the host, should order his wife's chosen meal when dining with her in a restaurant. I dine frequently with female business acquaintances who are acting as the host and paying for my meal. More often than not, however, even at some of the very best of restaurants, and even though my female host has chosen and ordered the wine, the waiter later shows me, the male, the bottle and invites me to taste it. Presumably, this is incorrect. Usually, when this happens, I will remind the waiter politely that the lady ordered the wine and leave it to him to rectify this, I believe, mistake. On other occasions, when I know my host well, I will smile discreetly at her and, to save embarrassment to the waiter, nod in acceptance of the wine I heard my host earlier choose, and carry out the tasting. How would you react?

A *I hope with grace but firmness. Restaurants are one of the last bastions of old-fashioned sexism. There are, however, various little tricks that the male guest can perform to try and encourage restaurant staff to treat a female host with due respect. These include: gesturing towards the woman concerned when the waiter approaches you for the food order, wine choice or indeed when presenting the bill. All these areas are the prerogative of the host, regardless of gender. Although many women hosts do invite the male guest to choose and taste the wine, it must be said that this gesture is entirely within her gift and not that of a presumptuous waiter.*

This letter also shows how, despite the contemporary concept of our living in a global village humming with finance, business and information technology, our everyday social customs remain remarkably parochial, as anyone who works in a multi-national company can attest. Such a dichotomy is ably illustrated by language. For indeed, while English may still be the *lingua franca* of the international community, thanks to British imperial dominance in the eighteenth and nineteenth centuries, America's pre-eminence in the twentieth and the needs of international software in the twenty-first, linguistic conventions still retain distinctly regional resonances.

Q I am in a situation that is increasingly common. I work for a European Multinational Company, and English is the designated business language for it. However, as English is not the first language for most people, and although the ability of our European cousins to speak English is markedly superior to my ability to speak their language, I find that many light-hearted sentences are lost on them, and I am continually struggling to resist the temptation, born from frustration, to correct poor pronunciation and sentence construction. Should I simply refrain from comedy?

A *No, keep up the good work. This you can do without any accusation from the PC brigade of post-imperial, Anglo-centric hegemony, as English is the "designated business language" of your firm. Your colleagues and company should thank you, notably for improving communication, but also for keeping everyone amused, too.*

The office affair is another great source of speculation in professional life, proving that even in the most hi-tech environment, low-tech activities still go on. Indeed, it is well known that many an extra-marital affair is ignited in the office, with a passionate glance over the photocopier, working late into the small hours, and that well-known excuse of personal excess with professional pretentions - the business trip. Needless to say, the office affair demands a protocol of the utmost tact and discretion, from not only those conducting the affair, but those quietly witnessing it as well:

> **Q** I am throwing a party for my 50th birthday. I have invited 100 people, including two couples, the female of one and the male of another from work. I, and the other "work" invitees know that my two chums have been having an affair for years. The husband of my girlfriend and the wife of my male chum appear to be unaware of what everyone else knows. I decided to invite both couples because I thought that they would discuss it between them - the two lovers - and perhaps decide that one couple would accept and one decline, but I would leave the decision to them. However, both have accepted. Was I wrong to invite both - should both have accepted, and how do I cope with the result?

> **A** *No, you adopted the well-mannered and non-judgmental approach of inviting both in the official social units that constitutes their marital states. It was left to them to decide whether it was appropriate to accept. As they have done so I can only conclude that, after years concealing their affair, they are skilled at making sure that social events such as your birthday party are unlikely to be sullied by a scene.*

CHAPTER IX

THE WELL-MANNERED TECHNOCRAT

Those who enjoy dismissing or ridiculing manners and etiquette like to maintain that they are nasty forces of conservatism and reactionism: feudal warlords paralysing us in an anthropological aspic so turgid that we are too frightened to let it all hang out and enjoy ourselves.

Where this misconception comes from I cannot imagine. Like many such simplistic views, it is founded largely in prejudice and perversity, not an understanding of human evolution.

The reality is that we are the masters of manners, not the other way around. We, true to our human wish to organise and codify, ruthlessly edit conventions that are no longer useful, and are constantly redefining modern behaviour to ease the struggle of everyday life. Manners, rather like their distant relation fashion, adapt remorselessly to social change and our requirements as sophisticated individuals.

No other area better illustrates this than the on-going development of a code for the taming of technology. Discussions about *netiquette* are frequently found in the national press, and even the mobile telephone providers are producing booklets on mobile manners. The Luddites, of course, decry technology as a tool for de-humanising our lives and thus blunting our interpersonal skills, of which manners are but one aspect. They no doubt identify with Max Frisch's definition of technology: "the knack of so arranging the world that we need not experience it".

This equally misguided view is, of course, a naive and nervous over-simplification. The student of history only has to recall that when the telephone was first invented in the last century, its critics declared that it would destroy the art of conversation. Anyone who regularly pays the family telephone bill will know what a hollow prediction that was!

Mobile phones are probably the most contentious of modern technological innovations, because they intrude so much into our everyday social life. Attitudes towards them also display the delightful double standards of the chattering classes. Rather like the view that, while everybody else is a tourist, we are travellers, and there are far too many cars on the road apart from our own, we regularly dismiss mobiles as a menace but would be loath to give them up ourselves. Indeed, recent figures show the total number of people in Britain now owning a cell phone to be over twenty-five million, a staggering forty-two per cent of our population. Thus, in the light of this statistic, it would seem that the mobile telephone has made a social journey from pariah to indispensible accessory in one short decade.

Early on in the column I codified the rules of engagement for well-mannered mobile usage. This inspired a considerable amount of correspondence to the column:

Q I well remember your advice in a column several months ago to leave mobile telephones with the reception in a restaurant, who can then summon you if you have an important call. I recently sat in an expensive restaurant at the next table to a man who was obviously not one of your readers as his mobile trilled every few minutes. I rather wetly didn't protest: should I have done and if so to whom, the waiter or the offender?

A *Mobile phones are the rabbits of technological invention, going forward and multiplying in such numbers that those in the population who resist their useful charms are beginning to feel like a persecuted minority. However, standards should still be maintained in public places, where thoughtless use of these machines can be incredibly invasive and irritating. I would not recommend tackling the actual owner directly unless his behaviour becomes unbearable. Instead call over the manager and try to co-opt him into championing your cause with the offender. I wish you a less aurally-challenging New Year.*

But what of private places? When visiting, mobile telephones obviate the awkwardness of asking to use hosts' telephones and to receive calls while you are a guest. In this way the host's line is not constantly blocked by his or her guests' inane chatter. However, new problems inevitably ensue. One hostess who regularly gives large house parties complains that the constant trilling of guests' telephones reminds her of her girlhood which involved summers staying near a puffin colony. She should count herself lucky that her guests are obviously too *recherché* to have insidious ear-curdling jingles programmed as their ring. For this reason guests should always make their telephone calls from their room, ought to leave phones switched off most of the time and not carry them around as if they are currency dealers awaiting the opening of the foreign exchange market in Tokyo. Certainly, behaviour described in the following letter is not to be tolerated:

Q My wife and I had a guest for tea who took two calls on her mobile phone while she was with us. Both brought conversation and tea to a halt while we listened in uneasy silence. Can you advise on the etiquette of using mobile phones? I deplore my aural space being invaded on public

transport and in restaurants, and dislike my home being turned into someone else's telephone box.

Space does not permit my going into the ins and outs of mobile telephone use here. However, I can quite unequivocally say that your guest displayed very bad mobile manners. It is very poor form to take calls when in any sort of a social situation with others. She should have instead left her phone either resolutely switched off or on voice mail, thus giving you her undivided attention.

E-mail is another fascinating area of contemporary discussion. Its impact on both business and social life is huge. However, like many new technologies, it is still evolving its own set of rules, which are loosely termed *netiquette*. Most intriguingly, it also shows how society will adapt technology to suit its established mores. This is well illustrated by the fact that when e-mail, which hovers somewhere between a telephone call and a letter in the communications stakes, first appeared, its form was largely expressed without conventional syntax and spelling. However, as its usage has become more widespread and is thus often required to express more complicated ideas, rather than simple messages from socially-challenged 'netties', we now find a variety of styles ranging from the briefest of acronyms to English that Keats could admire if he tried very hard. All these variations can be viewed as correct, but the circumstances in which e-mail can be used, instead of conventional methods, is still open to much debate:

Q Is e-mail socially acceptable? A friend, wishing to acknowledge a Christmas gift, sent an e-mail message to my computer which arrived before Christmas Day. What should my reaction be? Should I applaud her mastery of the technology and be grateful that she was polite enough to respond to my gift (albeit prematurely), or should I suggest that matters are best dealt with by the use of a good fountain pen, black ink, good quality writing paper and the service of the Royal Mail? I am sending this to you by fax which I assume is perfectly acceptable for business, but not social correspondence?

A *E-mail is professionally suitable but not socially so, unless there is no alternative. Certainly in the case of run-of-the-mill thank-you letters for Christmas, birthday and wedding presents, and for spells of hospitality, there is still no substitute for a real letter written with a proper pen and sent through the post. Furthermore, much as speed is always of the essence with any sort of letter of appreciation, and here I suppose e-mail does score, to send one before Christmas is so prompt that it is positively precocious. Your feelings about faxes, which occupy a similar position to e-mail when it comes to manners of the written word, are spot on.*

And what of the thank-you letter, that most symbolic of social graces? Its reported demise is seen by many traditionalists as a parable of modern-day decline in manners. Personally I think that, much like Mark Twain's death, news of its extinction is greatly exaggerated. This being said, people are much more lax about sending them than they were. The habit of next-day despatch seems to be practised only by the most punctilious, and the telephone call, in many cases, has replaced the letter altogether. Now e-mail has joined the bread and butter stakes:

Q I have just sent my first thank-you letter, a bread and butter missive, by e-mail and I am plagued with doubt. Is this ill-mannered? Have I committed a serious modern social blunder? Should I have played safe via Peter, my trusty postman?

A *Probably. Quick, convenient and even addictive as e-mail is, it is still preferable to avoid it in the case of thank-you letters and go for a proper hand-written letter instead. This is not for any Luddite reason, but a beautifully written conventional letter simply denotes a greater investment of time and effort on the part of the sender, and is thus likely to bring more pleasure to the recipient. However, it should be added that an e-mail thanks is better than no thanks at all.*

So much for new technology: what about the older science? Television is now decades old but its impact upon domestic life remains massive. For all its obvious benefits, many people cite it as a cataclysmic catalyst in the collapse of children's social skills; children who seem, when not surfing the net, to spend untold hours goggling. The same is true of adults, particularly of the couch potato variety:

Q My sister-in-law and I think it is bad-mannered when our hosts keep the TV on when we are invited to visit them. It is very hard to converse when the person you are speaking to sits with one eye and ear on the TV. It annoys us when the person says "Just a moment I want to see this". You feel like leaving and wonder why you have given up time to compete with the "box". Are we being too fuddy-duddy for our own good?

A *No. Unless guests are expressly invited to a television supper, where nursery food is served on trays, it is disconcertingly ill-mannered for their hosts to attempt to watch television during the visit of friends. A host's undivided attention is the common courtesy of hospitality and should be observed always. Hosts who are worried about missing television, simply have to avail themselves of that cunning little modern invention - the video recorder.*

Finally the answering machine or voice mail (the latter term is not non-U, as some suppose, merely transatlantic). There will still be the odd Neanderthals in dark corners of the kingdom who refuse to make use of these useful telecommunication services. Happily, I do not know very many. However, I do know people who exploit their use to avoid proper inter-personal communications. This, as well as being cowardly, is bad manners. The same is true of being reluctant to return calls:

Q I have been trying to make contact with a friend by telephone. Unfortunately he has an answer-phone, which means that repeating the attempt may be seen as pestering him. However, I know that many people with answer-phones often don't get round to listening to their messages. I wonder whether I should ring up and, if intercepted by the answer-phone, leave no message. Is it rude to ignore an answer-phone?

A *Yes, it is rude to ignore communications left on answering machines. This being said, people can be very vague: often they listen to messages, don't bother to write them down, only to lose them in the ether of lost memory. This is inefficiency bordering on rudeness. In addition, the hardware, rather like facsimile machines, is not entirely fool-proof. I do think it is sensible to ring your friend in the hope of catching him rather than his machine. However, if you fail do not be tempted to leave further messages, as increasingly desperate attempts are un-cool and irritating. Write him a short letter instead saying you have been trying to get in touch. If this does not elicit a response maybe it's time to take a hint.*

CHAPTER X

SEXUAL DIPLOMACY

Modern Manners is thankfully not a conventional problem page. I leave the agonies of our genito-centric age such as sexual dysfunction, infidelity and embarrassing illnesses to others more suited to these agitations. However, there are times when the world of *Modern Manners* does very occasionally venture into the Elysium and the Hades of the nation's private world.

First and foremost is the rekindled role of gallantry in the post-feminist age. Until quite recently men complained that if they dared to show any old-style courtesy towards certain women that a rebuke was the response. Now this reaction seems as dated as swooning like a silent screen heroine. Today's woman, confident in her equal status with today's man, now enjoys the best of both worlds: a gender-free working environment and a social life in which she revels in small gallantries that make life nicer for both sexes. Hooray for common sense! However, confusion still reigns for many at the gender boutique of Millennial manners:

Q There is a dispute between my father and me. It concerns standing up when a lady leaves the table in a restaurant or at a dinner party. My father insists that, even in today's "modern woman" age, it is still correct to stand up in full when one's female companion leaves or returns to the table. Whilst recognising that this courtesy was once correct for my father's generation, my experience is that it can embarrass the lady in question, the non-participating other male diners and me. I recognise the sentiment behind this custom and therefore tend to hedge my bets. When a lady leaves or arrives, I tend to elevate the frame of my body several inches whilst keeping my backside firmly on the seat. I'm rather good at it, but feel vaguely ridiculous. Your considered opinion would be appreciated.

A *This, like so many aspects of modern manners, is fundamentally a generational issue. As a general rule of thumb, with women above a certain age it is still expected that men should stand up when they arrive at the table, when they leave, and at any time in between when they might make themselves temporarily absent. An exception to this rule is if a woman asks men not to rise, in which case her wish should be honoured. Young women are more ambivalent about the habit. When socialising with them it is still polite to stand up when they arrive and when they leave; this is because the former is a greeting and the latter is a farewell. However, many young girls claim to feel embarrassed by over-zealous leaping at other times, such as visits to the loo. This being said, it is never rude to stand up, quite the reverse as it is men who remain resolutely cemented in their seats who look boorish. The secret is to judge the company, the formality of the situation and, if in doubt, just raise yourself gently and briefly from your seat without actually standing up.*

Then there are areas that have only recently become accessible to women, ranging from traditional institutions such as the law and politics right across public life to, if recent governmental recommendations are enacted, gentlemen's clubs. Even going to the pub is now an activity fraught with the perils of sexual politics:

Q I arrived at the bar of a public house; there was a lady standing awaiting service with a vacant chair next to her. Assuming she did not wish to be seated, I decided to occupy it myself without first asking her. Having sat down I became somewhat anxious that my actions might have appeared ungallant. In this age of feminism I did not wish to appear patronising by offering her the seat when she had already inferred she did not require it, but would I have been more courteous to offer it to her before taking it myself? Would a better solution have been to leave it vacant, or even repair to the lounge to avoid any appearance of rudeness? I would much appreciate your advice on this delicate matter.

A *This is a delicate matter, but one that can be easily remedied with a little careful handling. All you have to do is to fix the seat in your vision, then ask the woman in question "May I take that chair?". She undoubtedly will acquiesce. Should you also wish to avoid the impression of mistakenly appearing to chat her up, then the chair should be moved away from her immediate territory.*

Territory is indeed the demarcation of modern sexual diplomacy. Sexual liberation may well have brought us a multiple choice of sexual desire and fulfilment, but like all benefits it has its cost-balances too. These include confusion, feelings of inadequacy and simple problems regarding who should pay for the date. Perhaps Stephen Fry is right in his book *Hippopotamus*, "Before permissiveness came in, everyone everywhere was at it like randy goats. But the moment the young started to insist on talking about it all the time, you couldn't get laid if you were a table at the Savoy. As soon as it becomes a right you can't bloody do it anymore. Self-consciousness, you see".

This self-consciousness and confusion often continues well into a relationship where traditional gender roles have often metamorphosed into a quagmire of murky conventions. Even the smallest domestic task is not immune to cultural questioning:

> Q My girlfriend came to stay with me recently and very kindly offered to iron my shirts. Unfortunately, this seemingly innocuous activity developed into an argument after she insisted in ironing a crease along the top of my sleeves. I was always brought up to believe that shirt sleeves should be devoid of creases. Can you settle the argument please?

> A *Yes. The grandest, indeed Royal shirt sleeves, are generally ironed without creases. However, this is pressing for purists and requires a proper sleeve board, tons of technique and a dab hand with the spray starch. Quite frankly, I think you should be grateful that your girlfriend is so willing in the domestic department; there are countless young men who would envy your position.*

It can even be difficult to pay compliments these days without appearing predatory to the PC police, who seem to be able to read the most sinister of implications into entirely innocent comments. As all sensible and sensitive people know, political correctness is no substitute for good manners and its imposition can often have hilarious results, as the following letter illustrates:

Q My young and beautiful daughter has recently followed the modern trend for embellishment and installed a silver navel-ring. My elderly and proper (male) neighbour would like to offer appropriate compliments, but is at a loss to know how. To admire earrings is one thing, but to peer myopically at a neighbour's daughter's midriff with a Jolyon Forsyte-like "Ah, very nice" doesn't seem quite right. Are manners of modern western etiquette are short on tradition for this situation?

A *They are, and perhaps for good reason. I think in this case it is sensible to remember the old rule that it is not polite to pass personal comments, particularly when the sentiment would be expressed by an elderly male about the appearance of a nubile navel. I don't think there is any necessity whatsoever for this elderly neighbour to comment, as there is no necessity to comment on earrings. If he thinks this particular adornment is attractive and feels confident that your daughter is displaying it in such a way that she would welcome a compliment he could say so, but I think it better to say nothing.*

There are, however, times when silence is not so golden:

Q How does one handle the delicate situation of appraising an attractive young lady with shapely legs below a short skirt that she has developed, on the back of one leg, a ladder in her stocking from the ankle to the upper calf which she has not noticed nor can see?

Say, "I think you have a ladder in your tights".

My response received a very mixed reaction from my public as the following letter illustrates:

> *I feel I must take issue with Mr. Morgan over his advice about telling a lady she has a ladder in her tights! Surely the correct thing to do (unless it is a close female friend or colleague) is to pretend one has not noticed? The lady concerned will find out quite soon enough if she is not already aware of the situation; what is she supposed to do about it, unless she is one of these very well-organised ladies who always carries a spare pair in her handbag (unlikely, in my experience)? I am reminded of a comment made by a Buckingham Palace spokesman when a guest appeared at a function in a similar dress to that worn by the Queen: "Her Majesty never notices what people are wearing". I am sure this is the correct response regarding ladders.*

That may well be the case in this sensitive area. However, I have long believed that tough love is sometimes the order of the day. It is, thus, often kinder to tell somebody if there is something wrong with their appearance, e.g. spinach on the tooth and skirts in the knickers, if they are able to rectify it immediately and thus spare themselves further humiliation.

In the last analysis, when we look at sexual diplomacy, I return, like many before me, to the words of Plato who espoused with his usual genius that "love lies with the lover and not with the beloved". This philosophy should always guide our manners in matters of the heart.

CHAPTER XI

PROSE PERFECT

ALF SCOFFLIN ESQ

SID GRIBBLE INVITES
YOU TO A DRINKS PARTY
AT HOME
ON MONDAY 21 SEPT
AT 6.30 PM

PBAB
METHS

UNDER
WATERLOO
BRIDGE

Modern Manners, as well as innovating new forms of behaviour, also records the development of many of our more timeless customs of national life. Pre-eminent in these are the intricacies of letter writing and customs concerning the correct styling of envelopes and invitation cards. These considerations may appear quaint in the brave new world of cyberspace and virtual reality, but in fact they are quietly consoling, as they show not only an appreciation of the timeless, but also what a cultural kaleidoscope modern manners are: how many of our oldest customs can exist happily alongside the most novel of developments. Most charmingly, the concern for writing with style displays our ongoing need as a society to get things right. In this way we are the true inheritors of Lord Chesterfield.

But what have been the most popular issues concerning the written word that have been aired in the early columns of *Modern Manners*? The most-frequently-asked question is deeply demographic and concerns the correct styling of widows. This dilemma occurs so frequently in our post bag that it could theoretically warrant an end note in every weekly column. Therefore, let me reiterate my advice from Chapter V: widows should always be styled with their late husband's first name and not their own, the latter practice being reserved usually for divorcees.

Marital status in the spring rather than the winter of marriage is also of much concern. Now that many women choose to retain their own name, either partially or entirely after marriage, considerable debate has arisen on the contemporary correctitude of maiden name usage. Some couples decide to deal with this issue by creating a double-barrelled name which uses both surnames. In this way, a Miss Susan Smith, when she marries a Mr. Bryan Brown, becomes Mrs. Susan Smith-Brown. Happily, one of our ancient enshrined rights is that we can call ourselves whatever we like. This is an easy compromise, yet somehow it lacks style and seems to go against the fashionable trend to dispose of double-barrelled names created in the eighteenth and nineteenth century. A more elegant approach is to adopt a double identity rather than a double-barrel, in which a woman uses her own name professionally and her husband's privately. Many women claim to enjoy the counterpoint of this double life which, although it may dismay the odd unreconstituted feminist, gives many modern women the best of both worlds. Moreover, as the following letter reveals, it makes correspondence much easier to organise.

Q My wife and I will shortly be moving house and we will be sending out the usual change of address cards. My wife is known by both her married name and her maiden name, and those friends and colleagues that know one of these names do not necessarily know the other. Is there an appropriate formula we should use on the card to show both her names, or should we use two cards to cover both my wife's styles?

A *The form is simply to commission two sets of cards, one for each constituency of your wife's life. To try and combine the twin identities will confuse, bemuse and create complications.*

Modernity aside, many people still seem to get into a flap with the old chestnut of how to reply to a formal invitation. Maybe the modern mind feels awkward with the artifice of the third person singular;

certainly the rules have been explored in every copperplate intricacy in the pages of *Modern Manners*. The 'at Home' question is a good case in point. It ran and ran to such an extent that I even had to print a *mea culpa* for a behavioural brainstorm I exhibited in a column. But what is the 'at Home' question, I hear you ask? In reality, there are two main issues. The first pertains to whether a man could correctly be 'at Home' on an invitation card. This is a convention in flux, as tradition clearly states that it is a solecism for men to adopt such a social status. 'at Home' is a woman-only prerogative and men should restrict themselves to the 'Request the Pleasure of Your Company' model. However, many is the millennium man who finds this pompous and adopts 'at Home' instead. But is this correct? The answer is not yet, but maybe soon.

The second aspect relates to the nuances of the reply. This, contrary to common opinion, takes two different forms depending on whether it be a 'yea' or a 'nay'. An acceptance would read 'Miss Bella Battle accepts with pleasure Mrs. Cynthia Hastings' kind invitation to....'; whereas a refusal would run 'Miss Bella Battle thanks Mrs. Cynthia Hastings for her kind invitation to dinner on Tuesday 4th June but is sadly unable to accept'. The reason for these twin modes is entirely practical: the different opening dispenses with the time-consuming need for the recipient to read the entire document to get its message.

Q I have a query regarding how to reply to an invitation. I believe the correct form to be, "Mr John Smith thanks Mr and Mrs Mason for their kind invitation to the wedding of their daughter Jane on xxday, xxth August and has great pleasure in accepting". However, I am unsure as to the form of sign-off. Should it be "yours sincerely, John

Smith" or some other form? The parents are sticklers for etiquette and I do not want to give the impression of being gauche.

A *There is no sign-off in the case of third person replies. The date only is written in the bottom left-hand corner.*

The 'Esquire' issue is also a subject of much debate. Once this epithet was reserved only for armigerous landowners but, in the last century, its use gradually was extended to all those in the professional classes. Nowadays, when the gentry can find themselves on social security and many plumbers are often richer than their middle-class clients, the use of 'Esquire' becomes ever more problematical. It nevertheless remains a compliment and, although today it is largely eschewed in the business arena, I always recommend it when a writer wishes to be nice to whomever he is corresponding with.

Q Please advise me on the correct modern way to address a letter and the envelope. I now receive letters with the envelope addressed, "Gus Plaut". Should it not be "Dr. G.S. Plaut" or "Gus Plaut Esq. FRCS"? The text often starts "Dear Gus Plaut", but I think it should be "Dear Dr. Plaut" or "Dear Gus". Every now and again I receive an official letter from a lady I have never met signed "Wendy Jones". How do I reply? Many ladies object to being addressed as "Ms. Jones".

A *You are quite right about addressing letters and envelopes correctly. Envelopes to men are still properly addressed as "John Smith Esq.". "Mr John Smith" is gradually becoming acceptable, but still lacks style. "John Smith" alone is neither correct nor stylish except when addressing Quakers. How to open a letter is governed simply by how well you know the correspondent. Thus a man you have never met is "Dear Mr Smith" and a friend, "Dear John". "Dear John Smith" is inappropriate in all instances. When replying to official letters from women who have not specified a prefix, there is no option but to use the grim appellation of 'Ms'.*

The above, however, is only the tip of an epistolary iceberg, made ever more treacherous by the politics of gender.

Q **How should one address a letter to a person of unknown gender who is known only by surname and initials? It seems to be an increasingly common practice for employees of banks and insurance companies to sign their correspondence, "Yours sincerely, N.V. Bloggs", or whatever. Is it rude to reply "Dear Mr or Mrs Bloggs"?**

A *There was once a commercial convention that this type of unembellished sign-off suggested that the writer was a man. Women usually either wrote "Mrs" or "Miss" in brackets after their names (slightly non-U), or typed their name preceded by title under their* *signature. This is no longer the case and the only safe solution is to use the styleless, sexless, but increasingly prevalent business form i.e. "Dear N.V. Bloggs".*

How the lip of the estimable Lady Troubridge (*the* doyenne of pre-war etiquette) would have curled at this advice. But she conceded, even then, that times were changing. "You will hear a great many people declare that the telephone and the typewriter have destroyed the art of letter-writing. They are partly right and partly wrong". If Lady T. was writing today she could, of course, add the arrival of e-mail communications as well. All these things, although they have not killed off the written word, have encouraged briefer, more succinct and more note-like methods in written communications. Thus we find that a dashed-off missive on a postcard is now thought acceptable as an expression of thanks, whereas earlier only an elegantly and ably-expressed letter would have done. This trend explains the ever-increasing popularity of the correspondence card, which, as the following letter reveals, has developed its own protocol.

Q **I know with postcards it is not customary to write "Dear So-and-so" at the top of the message: but what is the form with correspondence cards?**

A *Correspondence cards retain the same conventions as postcards. Due to lack of space, written frills are kept to a minimum. The only way that the postcard's style varies from that of the correspondence card is that the latter is always sent in an envelope.*

CHAPTER XII

STYLE STAKES

It was Francis Bacon who most memorably drew an analogy between manners and dress. "Behaviour is the garment of the mind and ought to have the conditions of the garment. For first, it ought to be made in fashion; secondly, it should not be too curious or costly; thirdly, it ought to be framed as best to set forth any virtue of the mind and supply and hide any deformity; and lastly, and above all, it ought not to be strait, so as to confine the mind and interfere with its freedom in business and action".

Bacon's words ring as true today as they did to the Tudors. They also possibly explain why *Modern Manners* receives so much correspondence on style issues. Notice I write style, rather than fashion. The former is more timeless in its appeal while the latter is altogether more transient. Moreover, fashion education is also ubiquitous thanks to glossy magazines, shop windows and the Internet, whereas style is altogether more elusive.

This is because style is hard to define and a challenge to achieve. It means wearing the right thing at the right time in the right place and by the right person to create a look which has an air of modishness, confidence and appropriateness. This holistic approach creates a person who is entirely *bien dans sa peau*. As Oscar Wilde, never one to be lost for words, said to Ada Leverson who met Wilde as he was released from prison: "How marvellous of you to know exactly the right hat to wear at seven o'clock in the morning to meet a friend who has been away". Poor Oscar suggests, quite rightly, that in the style stakes there is a place for everything and everything should be in its place. Nowadays this is, of course, more difficult to define than in the past when there were strict, unspoken codes about appropriate dress. Today, so many decisions devolve to the wearer himself as the sartorial signposts have become weathered by age. Moreover, many individuals whose style lexicon stretches from T-shirts to track pants to trainers find themselves at a loss when it comes to understanding the vocabulary of grown-up gear. Thus, when important events occur that require effort and style on behalf of the wearer, they are confused. Yet, they still want to look their best for the important rites of passage in life: certainly when the British do dress up, whether it be for a family wedding or a grand ball, nobody can touch us for the unpretentious sense of occasion we create with our appearance.

I am inundated with enquiries about how to dress for special occasions that predominate in my correspondence. These enquiries come in from all age groups and make nonsense of the misconception that the young just want to look scruffy. My experience suggests quite the opposite, as the following letter reveals:

Q We are a group of students at Cambridge, and are going to the Trinity College May Ball this year. The ticket says, "White Tie preferred". Please could you explain the differences between black tie and white tie? Also, are clip-on bow ties a total social *faux-pas*?

A *Black tie consists of a dinner jacket teamed with trousers decorated with a single row of braid, and worn with a soft-collared shirt and a black tie. It is sported at run-of-the-mill formal evening parties. Its altogether grander brother, white tie, is reserved for the most formal and splendid of gatherings, and comprises a black cut-away coat, matching trousers with two rows of braid, stiff 'boiled' shirt, a detachable wing collar, white marcella waistcoat and tie. Clip-on bow ties should never be worn with either.*

Much of the manners aspect of dress concerns itself with the mastering of minutiae. Every well-dressed man (and woman too) knows that it is in his details that the winner in the sartorial stakes distinguishes himself. This mastery of minutiae has been called polite dressing and harks back to a tradition started by Beau Brummel, probably one of the greatest style-setters of all time. It was he who established understated but immaculate tailoring as the benchmark for men's dress. He certainly would appreciate the following enquiry:

 I have always understood that provided one's arms are not raised above shoulder level, the waistcoat should not show below the cutaway of a tail coat. But these days one often sees more than an inch of white showing - particular offenders are singers on concert platforms - and frankly, to me, it looks very ugly. Was I wrongly brought-up, or have fashions changed?

A *You were not and, equally, they have not.*

The mastery of minutiae is not confined to dressing *au soir*. Such skills are invaluable throughout the wardrobe. The same is true of developing a nose for the winds of change that blow items in and out of fashion. The Windsor knot is a case in point:

Q I would be grateful for your views on the acceptability of the Windsor knot. Ian Fleming advises that Bond considered it "showed too much vanity" and was often "the mark of a cad" (From Russia With Love). John Steed in 'The Avengers' sported a Windsor but always with a cutaway collar. Do the royal origins indicate a degree of credibility?

A *I am with Bond here. The Windsor knot is out of favour following a gradual decline in its reputation during the past half-century. Its royal provenance did much to establish the fashion initially but, rather like the eponymous Duke's contribution to statecraft, its legacy to the well-dressed man is limited. The only collar shape that it works with is indeed a Steed-style cutaway, but I would prefer to see a chunky four-in-hand knot instead.*

How to dress for weddings is also one of the great contemporary cross-roads where fashion and innovation meet manners and convention. As one of the last great dress-ups in our national life they provide people with a rare opportunity for sartorial self-expression on the grand scale. In addition, thanks to recent changes in the law which permit secular weddings at licensed premises other than register offices, and a fashion for ever-later weddings that span the night-time as well as the daytime hours, weddings have recently created a climate of diversity and, consequently, confusion:

Q We have been invited to a wedding in September, in this country. The invitation is for five o'clock at church and afterwards dinner and dancing at the bride's house. It does not seem to be black tie, as it is not mentioned on the card. I intend to wear an afternoon suit with a hat for church. Would it be appreciated to return to our hotel to change into a smart dress? Should I stay with my suit for the evening festivities? Or should I go to church with a dressy outfit which would be appropriate for both? I would prefer, of course, the first solution.

A *I suggest you will be cutting it fine if you attempt a change at your hotel. Why not take your inspiration from the recent wedding of Prince Edward and Sophie Rhys-Jones? Although I would not recommend your turning up in a long evening dress at a country church, you could go in an evening-ish dress worn with either a coat, short jacket or pashmina shawl, to render your appearance more suitable for church. Complete the look with a head-dress (feathers are very fashionable) rather than a hat.*

Issues can often become even more confusing with what to wear to second and even third weddings - events which, as yet, do not receive the full panoply of ecclesiastical approbation:

Q I have been invited to the Blessing of a wedding. (The wedding is earlier in the day at a registry office as one of the participants is on their second marriage). The Blessing is being held in the chapel of one of the larger Oxford colleges and is followed by an afternoon reception. Normally, I would always wear morning dress to a wedding. However, what is the correct dress for the Blessing? Morning dress or suit? If the latter, do I run the risk of appearing too much like Blair, Brown and others who eschew formal wear?

A *Let's not emulate them. Blessings tend to follow the same dress rules as a wedding would, particularly nowadays when their structure is often extremely similar to the actual marriage service. Yours, to me, sounds very much like a morning coat bash; however, a quick inquiry to the groom would resolve any dilemmas that you might have.*

Of course even though, as we discussed earlier, good style never goes out of fashion, there is quite predictably in the pages of *Modern Manners* much inter-generational debate about what constitutes contemporary modes in dress. Usually one generation automatically disowns the fashions of the previous ones, while often subconsciously adopting a re-run of styles of times they cannot remember: hence the fascinating revival of flares amongst teenagers. The following letter struck me as charmingly typical of this stylistic joshing across the age gap.

Q I recently took my family to the Stoke Newington Midsummer Fair near my home in North London. Now you may mock, but that is the nearest I may get all year to a country fair, so I chose to wear beige corduroy trousers with a three-button Crombie jacket, a light brown tweed, leather-button waistcoat, a quietly checked shirt (with rustic-design cufflinks) and a wide green silk tie with large white polka dots. My daughter, 14, who is never slow to criticise my dress, and whose appearance looks to me like a cast-off from the brothers Gallagher, complained that I should not wear checks with checks. I guiltily confessed that I was aware of that but feebly muttered that I was being post-modernist. This was scoffed at, (fortunately, she did not mock me for wearing silk with tweed). Do such things still matter to a gentleman and to those who should know?

A *Yes, they do. Your daughter's prejudice about checks is related to the well-worn City convention that striped shirts should never be worn with pin- or chalk-striped suits. The same prohibition does not apply to checks which can look very attractive if teamed in a stylish way. Judging by the obvious attention you pay to your dress I'm sure you achieved this. However, for many teenagers, their parents' appearance is often the source of limitless embarrassment. This, however, is usually owing to a surfeit of hormones in the off-spring rather than any sartorial shortcomings of the parent.*

CHAPTER XIII

MANNERS ON THE MOVE

It was G.K. Chesterton who opined "they say travel broadens the mind; but you must have the mind". How true these words ring nearly a century after they were written. All of us have witnessed the appallingly embarrassing behaviour of our compatriots on aeroplanes, at dusty airports during the holiday season and at resorts where well-behaved toes curl at the behaviour of some of our fellow countrymen. Many of these individuals leave their manners at passport control, obviously labouring under a xenophobic misconception that what you do abroad does not really count. I utterly take exception to this view, and always aim to behave in an exemplary way when travelling. This, happily, is an aspiration shared by many of my readers.

Pre-eminent in the polite minds of the correspondents of *Modern Manners* is behaviour on that most febrile of etiquette incubators: the modern aeroplane.

Here, high above the serenity of the clouds there often lurks a maelstrom of malevolent manners which can range from low-level irritants, such as tedious tinies, to psychotic drunks suffering from air rage induced by a lethal cocktail of oxygen-poor air supplied by penny-pinching airlines and a surfeit of complimentary booze. And then there is the so-called ticket to heaven syndrome which appears to be a millennial development of the mile-high club. Those of you familiar with such stratospheric shenanigans will recall that fliers overcome with lust normally repaired to the far from spacious confines of the loo. Now there have been reported incidents of couples practising the Karma Sutra with only a polyester travel rug to cover their modesty. Indeed, given such outrages, it is surprising that some people feel brave enough to travel at all.

Q On taking an aircraft seat can one expect to be able to make use of the armrest or is it first come first served? A later boarding passenger who has been allocated a middle seat often finds himself sitting down with the armrests on both sides fully occupied. Should one (a) make a polite request for elbow room to one of the adjacent seated passengers, (b) wait until one of them momentarily raises an arm and then discreetly acquire the armrest, (c) nudge gently to co-share an armrest or, (d) keep your arms to yourself until arrival?

A *The pursuit and acquisition of personal space has become an exact science of the air. The first solution would appear arch and is most likely to be ignored, thus causing unwanted ill-feeling. The third is likely to engender an even more negative reaction and the last is taking self-effacing sacrifice too far. Go for the second which perfectly encapsulates the democratic nature of mass air travel.*

It is these nuances that characterise best behaviour in the sky as the next letter illustrates:

Q When flying Economy Class how should passengers who require to respond to nature's needs overcome the obstacle of a sleeping passenger in the aisle seat? Manners seem to dictate that (s)he be left undisturbed; increasingly uncomfortable bodies demand otherwise. On a recent flight we drafted a note to a stewardess explaining our desperate situation and requesting her advice and assistance. However, between the writing and the delivering of the missive the sleeper stirred and we seized this half-open-eyed opportunity keenly and quickly. How should we properly have behaved if sleep had persisted?

A *In the first instance, it is sensible to try to ease yourself past the slumberer without actually waking him. This is possible in some economy seats, but requires delicate knee manoeuvres on the part of the person trying to get out. If he/she stirs awake, say simply: "So sorry to disturb you, but I need to....". However, in the cause of courteous directness, I would simply tap the sleeper on the arm and wake him/her briefly and apologetically.*

Ultimately, the polite traveller has to be the perfect technician of territory, a master of tact and a high priest of tolerance:

Q What is good form when reclining one's seat on a commercial flight, which necessarily involves an intrusion into what was previously the personal space of the passenger in the seat behind? Should one ask permission, give a polite warning, or (as the majority seem to do) just go ahead?

A *There is no reason to ask permission as seat-reclining is an accepted convention shared by all air passengers. However, before pressing the*

> *button, it is polite to acknowledge the presence of the*
> *traveller sitting behind by either smiling, or, as you suggest,*
> *offering a courteous alert.*

Then comes the destination which, as we all know, can often be a curate's egg of expectation and fulfilment. Bill Bryson, an incredibly astute commentator on our national mores, understands this dichotomy between what might be and what will be: "What an odd thing tourism is. You fly off to a strange land, eagerly abandoning all the comforts of home, and then expend vast quantities of time and money in a largely futile attempt to recapture the comforts that you wouldn't have lost if you hadn't left home in the first place". Language, of course, is another occupational hazard, particularly for the linguistically lazy British who view their tongue as a global comforter encircling the world, and who are often disgruntled to find that it doesn't always carry the day. It is at these times that we feel marginal inadequacies with our educational system.

Q My wife and I spend two weeks each summer staying at an up-market hotel in Ischia. The standards are such that the clientele remains almost exactly the same year in, year out. Over the years we have developed pleasant friendships with other guests from Rome, Munich and Cannes. They can all converse competently in English and I am embarrassed to say that I cannot reach a similar level of competence in their native tongues. Should I distance myself from these people until my current studies into their languages and cultures are complete? At the moment, I feel rather like a colonial dinosaur rather than a Europhile.

A Your concern alone shows that you are very much a Europhile. The mere fact that you want to improve your languages is much more impressive than the indifference of the average Briton, and thus will be appreciated by foreign nationals. There is thus absolutely no need for you to restrict your conversation and contact because you are no Petrarch, Goethe or Richelieu. Moreover, remember that nobody really expects the British to be good at languages. Our tongue, thanks to its adaptability, adoption by the world's last great super-power and its dominance of global technology means that, in linguistic terms, the mountain has to come to Mohammed. Secretly, those of other tongues are all rather jealous.

Of course, one doesn't have to travel to endure terror in transit. There are many vicissitudes that we experience at home both as travellers, motorists and, as the hapless victim of the next letter reveals, mortified passengers:

Q I recently had cause to undertake a long journey which would have been extremely difficult by public transport, and I gratefully accepted the offer of a lift with a friend of my parents, a distinguished clergyman. Unfortunately, we had not travelled many miles when I realised I was trapped with someone whose driving style was nothing short of homicidal. As we sped through an area with a thirty miles an hour speed limit at seventy miles an hour on the wrong side of the dual carriageway crash barrier, my driver appeared to be deep in prayer. The journey (lasting over three hours) was full of similar terrifying incidents and I arrived at my destination glad to be alive. Could you please suggest tactful methods of alerting a driver to the fact that he is petrifying his passenger without causing him deep offence?

A *Clergymen, because of their experience of giving sermons, are particularly receptive to incidents in the Bible that can be used allegorically to illustrate contemporary issues. I therefore suggest you scour both the Old and the New Testaments for an early traffic transgressor. Sadly, my somewhat sketchy knowledge of Scripture can't suggest a suitable subject, but I am sure that one exists and certain that if clearly extrapolated in letter form it would be very effective.*

It transpired that such a Biblical precedent does exist; *Modern Manners* was treated to a mail bag of biblical proportions from theologically-minded readers. The following delightful letter is typical.

The reference required by your correspondent with the dangerous clerical chauffeur is 2 Kings 9:20. This reads: "Again the sentinel reported, saying, 'He [the messenger] reached them, but he is not coming back. It looks like the driving of Jehu son of Nimshi; for he drives like a maniac'." (New Revised Standard Version: AV has "for he drives furiously".) This reference is sufficiently well-known in church circles that an inquiry as to whether the cleric took lessons at the Jehu School of Motoring should do the trick.

Chapter XIV

A Mad Miscellany

Finally, if not an encore then at least a delicious dessert: this short selection of very diverse letters that do not easily fit in to specific chapter headings, but are too priceless not to print.

Q As a dog owner, I regularly make use of "dog loos" in parks and other public places. When in the vicinity of these facilities I often meet other dog owners either going to or coming from them. Is it appropriate to give a cheerful greeting and perhaps to acknowledge their mission and its common purpose with mine, or should one follow the usual custom with similar human functions of pretending such things do not happen?

A *Such gentility is unnecessary in the animal kingdom, particularly in the case of dogs which have a propensity to leave unpleasant evidence whenever they get the opportunity. No, behaviour at the "dog loo" must be friendly and should positively bristle with canine chumminess. After all, anything that encourages the use of these facilities is a boon for dogs, their owners and the rest of us.*

Q Recently, while staying at my home in south-west France, I was invited to a supper party with English friends of mine nearby. Since my house does not have running water or electricity, I asked my hosts upon arrival whether I could use their shower. They showed me into their bathroom and left me with a fresh towel, telling me to "make myself at home". On drawing back the shower curtain, I found my hostess's underpants and bra hanging from the shower. My quandary is this: should I have replaced the bra and pants after my shower in exactly the same position as I found them, or should I have left them on the heated towel rail? I do not know my hosts well enough to feel that I could discuss the matter, but at the same time I did not wish to cause offence. In the event, I replaced them as I found them, after showering. What would have been the most appropriate action?

A *You did the right thing. Minor embarrassments should always be glossed over gracefully. Furthermore, as no doubt your hostess's underclothes contained elastic, had you put them on the hot rail you might have run the risk of bringing a whole new meaning to the word "smalls".*

Q There has been a long-standing difference of opinion in this household. Which is the correct way to hang lavatory paper? Is it to let the paper run down the wall or to allow it to hang over the top of the roll and down? Our friends have now become involved in this matter, the most learned of whom suggests 'top to bottom' is the rule to follow. Can you please advise?

A Your sage of the small room is entirely right with his "top to bottom" configuration.

Q Both my friend and I are avid computer and board game players. One particular car racing game automatically saves fastest lap times, of which I am the record holder on most courses. He is coming to stay for a few days in the future. What is the correct etiquette for such an occasion whereby he wishes to race me on my own computer in my own home? Should I, the host, allow him to win, and lose graciously yet purposefully, or do I defend my records with all the warrior instinct I can muster? Are there different forms of etiquette for board and computer games, and with games that rely on skill (such as chess) as compared to luck-based games? I would be most intrigued as to the actual answer as this will help the host's moral conscience immeasurably.

A Computer games are governed by the same protocols that regulate other competitive social activities, whether they be tennis or tiddly-winks. Thus it behoves a thoughtful host to give his guest a good game and not allow notions of self-effacement to overwhelm those of sportsmanship. The only possible exception to this rule is perhaps with the very young or the exceedingly old, who may benefit from a little confidence-boosting.

Q What is the most polite procedure when walking one's dog either on a lead or in an obedient frame of mind, one meets another owner with a dog which insists on following one's own? To stop is often to invite an unwanted conversation while the canines become embarrassingly intimate, but to walk quietly on risks distancing the other dog from its owner, who must then resort to unheeded and humiliating shouts, which become louder the further one walks away. This, of course, makes stopping less and less attractive. How is the situation best dealt with?

A *By swift action you will quickly curtail this canine* contretemps *which, like many similar incidents, is caused by animals being off their leads. Turn smartly to the other owner and say: "I think it would be a good idea if you would kindly put your dog on a lead. I'm afraid my mutt has a tendency to 'sort out' other dogs." The owner of the assailant, fearing his pampered pet might be in for more than just a sexy sniff, should have his dog out of the way before you can say "fetch".*

Q Early one morning this summer, I woke to the sound of rainfall. I suddenly remembered that the down pipe from the roof guttering was disconnected from the water butt, and I rushed outside. I had to stand on tiptoe with arms outstretched to connect the down pipe, and was thus spread-eagled facing the side of the house when I heard milk bottles clinking by the door: the milkman on his delivery round in the half-light of dawn. On hot nights, as this had been, I don't wear any night clothes, and had failed to get dressed in my rush to collect the rainwater. In my nakedness, I failed to greet the milkman with my customary, cheerful "Good morning". Instead, I froze, hoping he wouldn't notice me. I wonder if I have offended him - or if I would have by acting in a more extrovert and up-front manner.

A *Just as the well-trained butler always feigns complete indifference should he catch his master, mistress or others* in flagrante delicto, *on the loo, or stark naked, the form of somebody in your situation is to behave as if fully clothed. You should have merely turned your head to the milkman (perhaps not the rest of your body to spare him a full-frontal assault so early in the morning) and said a bright "Good morning". I suspect he would have regarded such a reaction as less unusual than the response you describe.*

Q At a recent theatrical production, it was my misfortune to sit next to a gentleman who felt it necessary to sing along with the more familiar musical numbers. He also felt it necessary to noisily munch through a box of chocolates. The gentleman and his companion discussed points of the production during the dialogue. I did not wish to spoil their evening by commenting on their behaviour, but they were indeed spoiling mine. I also did not wish to move seats as the house appeared to be full and it would not have been easy to do so. I would be grateful if you would advise on what to do in such situations?

A *How incredibly irritating. Unlike you, I am brutal in my treatment of selfish and noisy people who feel unable to distinguish between a public performance and a private viewing. At Covent Garden I have over the years perfected a three-step routine that rarely fails: first simply turn your head towards the offenders. If this doesn't work, turn your head and fix them with your eyes. If still no response then I am able to stage the loudest* shush *in the history of the lyric arts, thanks to several years of singing lessons. If this still doesn't work, which is highly unlikely, then simply intone "Will you please be quiet!". This sequence usually shames the offenders into silence and wins me compliments from other patrons who are either too timid or polite to do any of this themselves.*